THE
INNER CORE

THE INNER C♥RE

*Exploring the
Mystical Christian Experience*

Robert L. Marshall

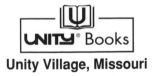

UNITY® Books

Unity Village, Missouri

First Edition 2001

Unity Books is part of Unity House, a publishing imprint of Unity School of Christianity. To receive a catalog of all Unity publications (books, cassettes, compact discs, and magazines) or to place an order, call the Customer Service Department: 816-969-2069 or 1-800-669-0282.

The publisher wishes to acknowledge the editorial work of Michael Maday and Raymond Teague; the copy services of Kay Thomure, Beth Anderson, and Marlene Barry; the production help of Rozanne Devine and Jane Blackwood; and the marketing efforts of Allen Liles, Dawn O'Malley, and Sharon Sartin.

Cover design by Gail Ishmael
Cover photo by CORBIS®
Interior design by Coleridge Design

The King James Version is used for all Bible verses, unless otherwise stated.

Library of Congress Card Number: 00-104699

ISBN 0-87159-266-5
Canada BN 13252 9033 RT

Unity Books feels a sacred trust to be a healing presence in the world. By printing with biodegradable soybean ink on recycled paper, we believe we are doing our part to be wise stewards of our Earth's resources.

DEDICATION

This book is dedicated to all of those who have shared with me the thrill, the frustration, and ultimately, the awe, of inner exploration. I am especially grateful to my wife Karrin for her enduring love and support through it all, my compatriots Fred and Merrilee who held the vision with me, and my daughter Lindsey Rose whose presence is a gift and assures me that our time of awakening is at hand.

TABLE OF CONTENTS

Introduction

THE INNER CORE

Every spiritual movement is composed of those who lead and those who follow. It seems that most of us find our place by becoming teachable. We study books, attend classes, and sincerely attempt to create the same patterns that others have outlined for us. Over time these patterns become sacred doctrines. The height of spiritual advancement is often measured by how closely one has aligned with these well-traveled doctrinal patterns.

However, within all vibrant spiritual movements there are a few who are not content to master the known patterns. They long for the realm not yet explored. They walk to the edge of their teaching and peer out beyond, just as the founders of their spiritual tradition did. Eventually, they step into the abyss and uncover a new, higher spiritual Truth. Though they may be criticized by those who police the boundaries of their religious movement, they become spiritual leaders, pioneering new inner realms. We call them mystics.

The mystic is simply one who studies the mysteries of life, the unseen, the unknown, and reaches out to experience these mysteries first-hand. Someone must step ahead of the masses to become the cutting edge of spiritual awakening. More and

1

more people then follow, until these realms become "normal" for large groups. Mystics work with the invisible until human beings awaken enough as a whole to see the potential they describe and accept it as natural. At this point, the mystic has once again forged ahead into the unknown next step. Thus the spiritual advancement of humanity progresses.

Every religion has within it an inner core of mystics who break new ground so that others may follow. World religions are like spokes in a wheel, with their mystics being those closest to the hub. The outer worship practices and names of each tradition seem quite distant. They lie far out on the spoke near the rim. Yet the mystics of different world religions are quite similar, having discovered the same inner spiritual principles and had similar transcendent experiences. The further we go, the more we realize there is only one Truth. There is only one God, no matter what we call Him/Her.

Jesus was a Jewish mystic, perhaps the greatest mystic who ever lived. Thus Christianity began as a mystical offshoot of Judaism. However, since Jesus' understanding and use of the higher invisible realm was so far beyond those who reached out to embrace Christianity, the Church placed him on a pedestal. They developed worship patterns for honoring his teaching, adulated him for his spiritual attainment, but shied away from truly following in his footsteps by colonizing these higher realms.

Christianity slowly became mired in "Churchianity." Most Christians stayed in the safe area: "Pray to God, worship Jesus Christ, follow the rules set by the church, and everything will be all right in the end."

Throughout all this time, there have always been a few who have kept the fire of spiritual exploration burning: monks in certain secluded monasteries, individuals with unquenchable thirsts for spiritual adventure, and small secret orders studying beyond the boundaries of majority opinion. Each chose to experience directly the inner realm Jesus taught so clearly. All carved whatever path they could and left their piece of the puzzle to humanity.

New Thought

During the mid to late 1800s and early 1900s, Christian mysticism entered into the public domain. Spiritual explorers like Mary Baker Eddy, Emma Curtis Hopkins, Charles and Myrtle Fillmore, and Ernest Holmes broke ground in areas of spiritual experience. Their personal encounters with the higher realms inspired others to move beyond doctrines onto a quest for the doors to the spiritual kingdom in which Jesus lived.

These loosely knit New Thought groups grew into a major spiritual movement. The emphasis on spiritual experience began to seep into Christian doctrines everywhere. The heralding of a higher Self within each human being was embraced by psychology. Science pursued the power of positive thinking, expanded powers of the mind, and the development of the higher human potential. Everyone began to enjoy the fruits of the mystical journey.

Human consciousness has begun to move swiftly now. The Truth taught by New Thought teachers is no longer the treasured pearl of a few, considered strange and far out by most. New Thought is rapidly becoming the popular philosophy of our time, regardless of religious affiliation.

Humanity has stirred into wakefulness. What was once cutting edge has become accepted norm. With this new acceptance has come a realignment of energies within the so-called Truth movement. Many Truth students have turned to the monstrous task of creating vehicles for training everyday people in the basics of spiritual development.

Marketing has become the byword. How can we package our cutting-edge awareness more attractively so as to reach the most people? Valid and demanding as this need is to serve, another problem requires our attention. When cutting edge becomes normal (as it should), who is stepping beyond to the new cutting edge? In an era when mysticism as we know it is becoming the safe zone, who is exploring the new mysticism, the new unknown that lies before us?

Every truly successful company has a research and development department to make sure that marketing has something up-to-date to work with in the future. Teaching the standards is important, but without spiritual exploration, stagnation will set in.

Human-consciousness evolution has accelerated. No longer can a handful do the exploration while the rest follow. To keep pace, more and more people must carry their quest beyond the basics, beyond the limits of what is known, and bring back their findings for a ravenous humanity to devour and assimilate.

If you have been thirsting for more, feeling the need to "experience" something deeper, and have the courage to try to do the things that Jesus did, then you have been given the invitation to join the inner core of spiritual explorers who will cut new paths inward into the higher realms.

Practical Mysticism

If you choose to accept this invitation, you will have begun the adventure of your lifetime. You will need to develop some new skills. There is no one to tell you how to go where you want to go or what you will actually find. We can give suggestions as to how to start on a project and some pointers on how to develop your own techniques and practices. However, no one but the Masters have gone down the path as far as you will go. What you discover will excite even those you call teachers.

As a young man, I learned to sail by reading several "how-to" books on the subject. I learned the parts of a sailboat and the theory of sailing. I also learned how to make all kinds of maneuvers in my mind. Though I began to feel that I had a mastery of sailing, I frustratingly yearned to actually put my hands on the boat.

Finally, I acquired this prized possession and put it in the water, sure I would sail like a pro. I found, immediately, that doing it was a lot harder than learning the philosophy. In fact, transferring my sailing expertise from mental understanding to actual experience was one of the truly challenging experiences of my life.

It is the same with spiritual things. Many believe that if they read enough books, gather enough spiritual knowledge, and master the philosophy, they will become illumined. Reading inspires you toward your goal, helps you to stay centered, and possibly gives you some suggestions to start with. Reading takes you to the door of a spiritual adventure but is a poor substitute for the actual experience.

If you are to join the inner core as a spiritual explorer, you will have to take your religion out of the section labeled "philosophy" and move it into "do-it-yourself." We don't want to hear what you believe to be true. We want to hear what you've found by actually going there.

There's a big difference between professing that "faith moves mountains" and moving them. When you've actually done it, we want you to tell us how you finally accomplished the task. Even if you fail, the jewel may be in what you encountered trying—what worked, what didn't, what seemed to help, and where you lost it.

Mystical exploration has always involved group effort. No one can do it all, so we glean as much experiential information from one another as we can. Someone eventually breaks through.

As a spiritual explorer, you must first master weeding out useless, unproven philosophy from experiential information that enables you to "do" something in a spiritual area. To this end, we are always looking for practices which we can work with to encourage an experience of the Truth which we accept.

If no practice is presented, consider how you might give this principle concrete expression in your life. Create an activity which uses the principle or a meditation which concentrates on the principle until it goes beyond a mental concept and becomes an experience, something happening so strongly in your feeling nature that it overshadows the original mental picture.

Scientists prove theories by creating experiments that physically demonstrate the use of the theory. It is not accepted as scientific fact until other scientists in other areas can follow the instructions of the first scientist and come up with the same results.

Admittedly, mystical exploration is a little harder to tie up into a neat package. Yet our results should be provable by others who follow with dedication the same practices we develop. In fact, those who follow our instructions should get there a bit faster since we can warn them of the pitfalls and urge them toward the most effective approach.

SPIRITUAL EXPLORATION

An expedition requires someone or several people to play the role of "point," scouts to go out ahead of the main group and report back about the terrain. These pathfinders explore by trial and error the most effective route and urge the main body to travel that way to avoid the dead ends.

Humanity is on an expedition in search of the lost kingdom of heaven that the ancient mystic Jesus Christ found, explored, and taught. He showed us where it lies and is available to help us retrace his steps. But the expedition still needs scouts to forge ahead into this experiential terrain and determine where it is easiest to break through the limits of our group consciousness.

The speed of our expedition has increased. We sense freedom ahead and are quickening the pace. Human-consciousness evolution has reached a frenzy. In earlier times a few mystics exploring ahead kept humankind crawling along. Now we must cut paths in a thousand different directions, because the people of the Earth are ready to follow.

It's a glorious time to be alive. Generations from now, our era will be remembered as one of spiritual pioneers settling the new frontier. But we haven't completed the challenge yet. We've just begun, and now the rules have changed. We can't depend on a few to lead. We need a legion of spiritual explorers to cover the territory. I hope you are willing to be one of them.

When faced with spiritual challenges, Unity cofounder

Charles Fillmore was quoted as declaring, "I will go straight to headquarters." He then proceeded to sit in the silence each day until Spirit revealed the answers to him. In this tradition, a number of years back, I set about a process referred to as "opening the heart."

OPENING THE HEART

I became aware that there were certain spiritual experiences which I was missing. I was told that they lay in the area of the heart but was given very little guidance as to how to reach them. Feeling at a loss as to what to do, I simply started concentrating on my heart center and using affirmations.

At first, I seemed to be getting nowhere, but finally, I started feeling a slight thrill that I would later declare was heart energy. The process got speeded up immensely by the advent of an emotional crisis that shattered my life. As I struggled to keep my ideals and my sanity in the midst of a crumbling world, something popped open, and I started experiencing beauty to a depth that seemed almost to hurt.

Grabbing my new leverage with both hands, I devised all sorts of practices to keep experiencing beauty everywhere I went. I redoubled my efforts to meditate on the heart center, using sound, affirmations, visualization—any technique I could come up with. As a result, I became able to generate an energy in my chest at will. That energy would change the way I related to people and events.

For the next five years I explored the application of this energy in every area I could. I learned to change emotional states, to see beauty and deeper purpose in everything, to reach out and touch people or things with my heart, to know the inner essence of people and patterns of growth. The whole realm of intuition opened, and my spiritual path went from black and white to color.

The further I reached, the wider the unexplored vistas became. I was overwhelmed by the realization that I would never be able to explore even a fraction of the immense territory which lay through the door called "the heart." One entire lifetime would not be enough. And other spiritual areas were beckoning to me. I wanted to look into these areas also.

About this time a friend came to me describing experiences that were happening to her. I recognized them as heart openings and excitedly told her, "I know some practices that will speed this process along." I'd spent five years wandering—trying this or that until I hit something which worked. I was able to share with her the fruits of my labor. I gave her the practices that had worked best for me in each area of development.

A little over two months later she returned, thanking me for the guidance and having gained some measure of mastery in each of the areas we talked about. What had taken me five years, she covered in a few months. She didn't have to walk down blind alleys and struggle in darkness. Someone who'd already done that gave her a map.

I remember wishing that there was someone who had spent those last five years working in one of the areas I'd not covered, who could show me the shortcuts. After all, I wasn't sure I had five years to devote to every spiritual quality I needed to develop, especially in light of the fact that my five years had only brushed the surface of unexplored areas within the heart.

It was here that the dream of the Inner Core took form. I began to realize that I didn't have time to pioneer every area.

The process is too slow. But I could pioneer one area or a handful of areas in my lifetime and teach others what I'd learned. They could also pioneer and teach me what they learned. A group could accomplish what no single one of us could.

WORKING TOGETHER

I believe that Christ consciousness is attainable by us in this generation. Recently I've come to believe that the path is set up so perfectly that to reach the top, we cannot do it alone. We must reach beyond our separateness and work together as one.

I don't have five years to devote to every aspect of Christ awakening. But if I spend five years on one area and you spend five years on another and someone else covers yet another aspect, and then we teach one another, the whole group and each of us within the group travel farther than any *one* of us could hope for. Together, we can present quite a nice chunk of consciousness to the next generation. They will soak it up as if it had always been easy and will cut paths into areas beyond.

THE INNER CORE SUPPORT GROUP

In an era of support groups for every malady a human personality can fall into, I urge you to gather others of like aspiration and form an Inner Core support group for spiritual explorers. Let's have support groups for those whose spiritual quest goes into potentials only hinted at so far. It's time to quit hiding unexplained spiritual happenings in the closet because people might think us strange. Ask around. You'll find there are others like you to share the journey and the work.

Our spiritual traditions cover the basics well. But when you are hungering for more, don't leave your church or spiritual family looking vainly for higher teachings. One mystic put it like this, "Be firmly rooted in your tradition, but become its cutting edge." Running from place to place will not provide the shortcut to enlightenment. Stand in one place and dig in. Quit looking for the way around the work and start doing it.

Years ago I looked out across the field of leaders within my spiritual tradition, planning to choose one to emulate. Some wonderful names were on my list. Yet, as I went through them, there was always a reason or two that I should not totally pattern myself after them. After disqualifying the finest names in the movement for this reason or that, I sadly found myself at a loss. Whom shall I pattern myself after?

I retorted to myself: Well, Jesus Christ, of course. Yes, but I was hoping for someone a little more tangible—someone in between Jesus and myself.

I usually don't hear voices, but occasionally a thought comes through so clearly that it could be a voice. This was one of those times. *Become the spiritual leader you seek!*

The thought-voice was forceful and direct, leaving no room for questioning, and it rocked me. I soberly contemplated the assignment for a moment and then had to laugh. Of course! This is the instruction for anyone who travels the path. Eventually, each of us must stop looking for someone else to lead the way. We each must take our turn at the front.

If this is your realization, that it is time to walk to the edge and put your ideals to the test, you will take comfort from others who have accepted the same assignment. They will be all around you, and you need the power that bonding with them will provide.

Jesus said, "Where two or three are gathered together in my name, there am I in the midst of them." Over and over we have proven the spiritual power of gathering together in an effort to express the spiritual principles that Jesus demonstrated so well. Small prayer groups with each person praying for the desires of the others have proven almost magical. Miracles happen. The bonding of the group goes deep. There is power in such a group.

What we are creating here in the Inner Core is a prayer group with an even higher objective. Instead of asking the group energy to draw to us our earthly needs, we are using the group energy to draw forth from each of us some expression of the Christ Self. You will be sharing your deepest, most sacred experiences, your frustrations and failures in reaching toward the highest of ideals, your hard-earned successes, and the map of how to reach them. As you can see, this group could become very powerful in catapulting you forward. Treat this gathering with the utmost of reverence.

Much of this power will be dissipated if you lose focus. Our objective is to do the things that Jesus did, to follow in his footsteps in a very concrete way. To turn philosophy into action and, in a sense, religion into science. We are offering ourselves as living laboratories for the creation of the expanded human being. We aspire to Christ consciousness and are willing to get there one quality at a time, if need be. We abandon the fear that has held us within safe boundaries. If we are children of God, it is time we figure out how to do the things children of God do and not just settle for baby steps.

THREE PITFALLS

The first pitfall to watch for is debate. Intellectual debate can be invigorating, but there are plenty of places to pursue philosophical discussion. This group is not about "thinking." It is about "doing" and "being."

Keep centered on experiences and the practices or possible steps that could lead to them. Share exactly what you've encountered in your research project and the realizations you've come to that could prove helpful to others in getting results. Brainstorm other approaches. Report your blind alleys so others in the group can avoid them. Journal breakthroughs so others outside your group may eventually benefit. Then pray together and know for all those in the group that Spirit will guide them to success.

The second pitfall to avoid is allowing the group to degenerate into a counseling session. This is deadly to a prayer group of any kind. The emphasis shifts from the Divine to the human, with the resulting loss of power.

The members of your Inner Core group will become intimate friends. You will want to share your daily pleasures and traumas. You should, but not at the official gathering. Let that be strictly an experience of Divine Power in action. Share learning experiences and the accompanying realizations, but be sure it serves the higher Self when you do.

Bible teacher Dr. Herbert Hunt used to start every session with the statement, "Jesus Christ is the head of this class." It's worth remembering, especially when the third menace, "inadequacy," sets in: I don't have anything to offer . . . I don't know how to get started . . . I keep hitting a brick wall . . . Everyone's having experiences but me.

When you are sure you're not up to the job and there is no one to show you how, remember that Jesus Christ is the head of this class.

Yes, we are forging into generally unknown territory, but

it's a realm that Jesus understands intimately. Hold to the knowledge that his presence will guide you (seemingly haphazardly) onto a path that will take you where you need to go.

If that leaves you a little unsure, possibly your relationship with Jesus Christ is worth a research project. However, Jesus told his followers that after he left, the Spirit of Truth would come and teach them everything they needed to know. This same Spirit of Truth sets up the entire learning curriculum that life provides. Trust life to show you a path. If you endure in this knowing, it always does.

There is a third pitfall the group must avoid. Let's call it "pride." When spiritual experiences start happening in abundance and breakthroughs push us far ahead of our expectations, some will face the "guru ego test." People will admire you for what you have attained under God's direction. Messiah-hood is enticing. Sidestep this one by keeping things in perspective.

Recently someone told me her friend now believed himself to be an "old soul." I responded that I had that feeling about myself: "I feel I've been around forever, but I'm not sure it's anything to be proud of. It's kind of like bragging that you are a 20-year-old in the 5th grade. I'd much rather be a young soul moving right along."

There's always a different perspective. Don't be so quick to claim your laurels even when wonderful things begin to happen. Pace yourself. There's a long way to go.

Chapter 1

THE PATH OF MYSTICISM

You are a mystic! You wouldn't even be reading these words if you weren't interested in the study of the invisible mysteries of life, the unknown that lies just beyond our reach. Yet if you are to immerse yourself in mysticism and not just dabble in phenomena, you will have to first determine your level of commitment. Pioneering is not easy. You will turn back before a major breakthrough if you are not totally committed.

I once watched a documentary of a young woman who was one of the top rock climbers in the country. This film followed her on a solo climb up a several-hundred-foot crevice. Much of the climb she made by stretching her legs across the narrow gap with one foot on each side. Keeping pressure on the opposite slabs, she would inch her way up between them. She had a safety rope around her waist and every so often would secure another clasp to the stone wall, so if she fell, the rope would break her fall.

About two-thirds of the way up, the rope became tangled at the bottom. No matter how she tried to dislodge it, the rope remained stuck and would stretch no higher. A dedicated climber would have reluctantly begun a descent. Instead, she untied the rope from her waist and continued;

near the top, the gap became larger. She had to stretch across with hands on one side and feet on the other. I breathlessly applauded her courage and commitment as she cleared the top.

At the time the climber untied the rope, the stakes went up. Before, the climb was something she was doing with her life. After, it *was* her life! That is the commitment required to unlock your piece of Christ consciousness and give it to the world. It is not enough to be a dedicated student. You must have committed your whole life to God.

Once a teenager excitedly told me that she had just dedicated her whole life to God. It had been an important turning point for her, and she knew exactly when it happened.

As I contemplated this, I realized that in my own life, I could not pinpoint an exact moment when I completely committed my life to God, but it was true nonetheless. For me, it had come subtly, piece by piece, until that commitment was the deepest driving force of my life.

This is the time to ask yourself how committed you are to surrendering your life to God to be used as a spiritual experiment for the betterment of humankind. If you are unsure that you have ever made this total commitment before, you can proceed by making it now. You can untie the safety rope around your waist and abandon your life to serving God's purposes wherever they may lead you.

THREE COMMITMENTS

Professing commitment and expressing commitment are often somewhat different phenomena. Consequently, I suggest that those who wish to join the ranks of the spiritual explorers make concrete commitments in three basic areas. In this way, you will open the doors to success. Unwillingness to make a commitment in these areas generally means you do not have sufficient stamina to endure very far down the path into the unknown.

The first area of commitment is *service*. Jesus stated quite clearly that anyone who would become great must learn to serve (Luke 22:25-27).

Beginning-stage Truth students center upon taking as much enlightenment as they can. "Feed me, feed me," they cry—like baby birds. As they decide they are more advanced, they start roving from place to place seeking something they haven't heard. They migrate from church to church, workshop to workshop, looking for the magic key. Each time they leave, they claim they have "outgrown" this church or that teacher.

What they fail to realize is that all the higher lessons come when we quit coming to "take" enlightenment and come to give something. You serve when you quit demanding that spiritual gatherings teach you something new. Rather, you go to give support, to help in any menial way you can, to be part of the group consciousness and, thus, give yourself to the group. Teaching is a way of serving, but be careful because it also has a way of making you feel important. If you are doing it for the adulation, you are still taking.

Choose a church or service organization and volunteer to help in some way, even silently giving your energies if no outer vehicle presents itself. In lieu of an organization, you must create a special plan for serving others all on your own.

The second area of commitment is *finances*. I include this because so many would rather leave it out. If any area of your life is too secular to be committed to God, you are not totally committed. You are starting down the river in a leaky boat.

Make sure you have discussed finances with God. Make a commitment between you and God (no one else) as to how you will share your abundance with God's physical work on this earth plane. I tithe to be clear on my financial commitment. You must come to whatever agreement you and God can arrive at. Then fulfill it. Don't be too tight here. You are asking for God's full commitment to you on your journey ahead. You will receive the commitment you give.

The third area of commitment is *integrity,* to explore and teach what you learn. You are making the commitment to choose an area of consciousness. Dedicate your energies to it until you have tapped its hidden potentials, and condense all you have learned into a package that can be presented to others.

This is the foundation block upon which Inner Core groups are born. Those who plead inadequacy and come to the group only to learn what others have found rarely last long. You are committing to work. Even as a rank beginner, you have much to offer if you fulfill your commitment to do spiritual work.

The Inner Core gathering is not a class or discussion group, club or fraternity. None of these carries the level of commitment we are seeking or the sacredness of its mission. Were I to give it a name, I would say that each Inner Core group becomes a *mystical order.* Each member is held together with the others of the group by the highest of spiritual values. Each is totally committed to the other's success in mystical exploration. Each is totally committed to putting his or her whole being into the spiritual work before them. Together, they are silently joining in consciousness with spiritual explorers everywhere. Remember the sacredness of the purposes you serve.

A MISSION STATEMENT

If one were asked for the mission statement of mystical exploration, it could be stated clearly by quoting one of Jesus' power statements: "I, if I be lifted up from the earth, will draw all men unto me" (Jn. 12:32).

A number of years ago, I affirmed this statement hundreds of times a day for six weeks. I was on a quest to know what it felt like to be the man who made this powerful statement. Day by day the words filled with energy and became richer. The meaning behind them expanded to include volumes that could not be recorded. It became utter joy just to speak them.

I began to grasp the mission. We are all united. One cannot rise without lifting everyone around us. We ask not to be lifted above other people but to be the channel through which everyone is lifted. We make the joyous realization that as we succeed, so does all humankind.

"Father, allow me to rise out of limitation, knowing that all humanity will be irresistibly drawn up around me. Let me do it for the whole." Through spiritual exploration, we carry on Jesus' mission of lifting humanity to new heights.

I suggest that you affirm an updated version of this statement, *I, if I be lifted up . . . will draw all **humanity** unto me,* until it resonates in your being. Use this statement individually, and use it as a group. It will keep you centered on your purpose.

As a mystic, you are a disciple of the Master, Jesus Christ. Jesus is the head of our mystical order. We need to explore the meaning of that disciple/Master relationship that is often referred to so glibly.

THE DISCIPLE/MASTER RELATIONSHIP

As a disciple, you have committed to follow in the Master's footsteps . . . to apply his teachings in every area of your life . . . to emulate his consciousness . . . to walk in his presence . . . to accept the challenge of doing the things he did . . . reaching and trying until you succeed . . . until you break through to the inner kingdom where he did his work . . . until you join his ranks as a Master, an awakened child of God, worthy of being called brother or sister of Jesus Christ.

Quite a tall order. Discipleship is not for the faint of heart. It is like in moving a mountain of dirt, you begin that monstrous task with the first shovelful. Then just keep shoveling.

In return for your commitment as disciple, Jesus is there as your example, your friend, and your teacher. His presence is available to you as you meditate and pray. Ask him to sit with you. He can merge with you when you don't feel up to the task at hand. His presence is with you in the difficult times. Truly, this disciple/Master relationship is worth cultivating.

Upon entering a committed spiritual path, the disciple is initiated into the ranks of the others who share the path. In the end, initiation is an inner experience that acts like a punctuation mark between one pattern of life and a new one. This mile marker may stand out boldly as with my young friend who knew exactly when she committed her life to God, or it may be so subtle as to be missed. For this reason, mystical movements celebrate initiation with outer traditions.

INITIATIONS

You may believe that you have never been through an outer initiation before. Yet that may be untrue. If you have ever joined a Christian church of any denomination or been baptized, you have received the first initiation into the ranks of those who follow Jesus Christ. Once again, let me remind you the real initiation took place within your heart when you made your commitment.

There are other initiations beyond that early one. When you accept responsibility in your spiritual family by serving or teaching, you accept a deeper commitment and initiation, though it may not be recognized in an outer way. Ordination is an initiation into the ranks of those who will serve God in a professional capacity, often by leading in a church structure. Thus ministers enter a brother- sisterhood of a particular path. Other mystical groups initiate aspirants in healing orders or agricultural orders (serving nature spiritually).

When you embrace the path of spiritual exploration, you are initiated into the ranks of all of those who have been spiritual pioneers—all of those whose goal is to expand and lift the consciousness of the planet, to serve the whole in this way. Essentially, you are initiated into the spiritual hierarchy.

Years ago, when I first heard the words *spiritual hierarchy,* something inside me responded with a joyous, "Yes!" In some form or other, all the great beings throughout the ages that have tried to lift humankind above animalistic drives to realization of our divine nature must still be working with the human-race consciousness of our planet. Their desire for the good of the whole would unite them. Add to them the angels and celestial beings serving the Earth and you have a massive hierarchy, all contributing at their level of awakening. Together, they are slowly guiding the ship of human consciousness toward a heavenly harbor ahead.

Jesus is at the wheel of this ship, but everyone is contributing a part to the whole. Beings incarnate in physical form must be part of this grand scheme of awakening, united with those beyond by that deep-seated desire for the good of the whole. Some stand out and are recognized. Others contribute silently—unheralded.

I remember as this vision took form in my mind's eye, desire leapt in my heart: I want to serve the spiritual hierarchy. Let me just be a pencil sharpener for the hierarchy, and my life will be full!

When we accept initiation into spiritual exploration as our path of service, we humbly join the ranks of all the beings of Light that serve this planet. To be their pencil sharpener is worth all the drudgery and work our path may create.

A FULL PAIL

Lillian is a good friend of mine who has been interested in altruistic ideals all of her life. She envisions a gentler world where the beauty of spiritual ideals dominates. Her path has taken her through a number of mystics and charismatic teachers. In each case, she has been willing to sit at their feet and do whatever they would tell her in order to live in that more beautiful reality.

A number of years ago she attended an evening lecture given by a mystical teacher. His presentation was so inspiring that she felt led to approach him afterward. She offered her enthusiastic appreciation of his words and finally asked for his guidance by blurting out: "I want to help the world. What should I do?"

The teacher looked deeply into her energetic and naive enthusiasm with compassion. He paused and then replied quite directly, "Before you can quench the thirst of the masses, your own pail must be full." He ended with a gentle smile and then turned to the next person waiting behind her.

In those few words, he had redirected her out of the fantasies of the spiritual path and into its realities. The task is not accomplished by simply catching the vision. All the enthusiasm in the world cannot replace good, hard work.

You who think you have come so far and are ready to embark upon the noble task of serving the world, recognize that your pail is empty. Only then can you choose wisely what you will put into it. Only when your pail contains something of worth can you truly serve the world.

Ask yourself: What will I put into my pail? In what particular area of consciousness will I do my good, hard work? It's often a difficult choice. After all, there is so much to choose from. How can I narrow it down? How can I determine what I need to work on most?

YOUR SPIRITUAL ASSIGNMENT

If we are serving the hierarchy with our lives, then surely we want our efforts to blend with the needs of the whole. We want an "assignment," something that is our particular contribution.

You have probably already recognized that God seems to be giving you assignments almost every day. People approach whom you can help in some way. You happen onto something that you have the skill to fix. You see the opportunity to create a little beauty. Life offers us these assignments automatically if we are looking for them. Your assignment for spiritual exploration is probably sitting right in front of you.

Realize that your assignment is to build a particular chunk of consciousness. As a group, we are building Christ into human awareness, block by block. You will meditate and integrate into your consciousness a certain higher energy or ability. You will take it far beyond the concept stage. You will build it into your guts until it is no longer something you think to do, but an energy you radiate without thinking.

TWO LOGICAL APPROACHES

There are two approaches you can take toward logically discovering your assignment.

The first is to consider what comes to you naturally. If healing is something for which you have a real affinity, maybe that's where you should begin. If you are already tapping into prophetic dreaming, consider refining the experience and dissecting its components until you can teach others how to experience the same thing. Something that is already partially developed may give you a jumping-off spot for diving into the depths.

The second approach is quite the opposite. After having spent more than five years on my heart, I took a sincere look at my consciousness and tried to determine where I was weakest. The logic was that to balance my consciousness I needed to develop something I didn't feel connected with yet.

Will was my strongest faculty. I'd worked with abundance and made some breakthroughs there. Though I was healthy, I realized I'd always accomplished it with will, not healing life. I didn't feel tightly connected to that life force that seemed to flow naturally through the lumberjack type of individual or the body-to-body communication that comes so naturally to some people. So I chose life force as my next assignment.

For those of you who find your assignment in your weakness rather than your strength, remember to be steadfast in your conviction to not give up until you succeed. It is a difficult task to develop a void in consciousness because you have little to start with. It can be tedious, even fruitless, for long periods of time. When you finally break through, you will know it was worth all the work. Even if you build only a meager flow of this energy through your life, things improve for you dramatically.

I worked with life force for months with no seeming success before I started to see small breakthroughs. Though my results seemed quite limited, I made some unusual discoveries that have proved valuable even to those who touch life force naturally.

THE UNIVERSAL ASSIGNMENT

If after all is said and done, you do not feel directed to any particular assignment, consider working on opening your heart center. This project is universal. Jesus presented to his disciples the path of the heart. Open your heart and everything else will flow quite naturally. Future assignments will come into focus. An open heart is the springboard to everything else.

Once you have contemplated the possibilities that lie before you, fall back and regroup. The exploration chosen is an "assignment" because it is God-directed, not self-directed. Do your homework. Examine your consciousness . . . your strengths . . . your flaws . . . what you are attracted to. Then consult God. Ask God to show you what to pursue or to confirm one of the choices before you. Be open, receptive, and willing to do the will of God, whatever it might be.

It is time to go into meditation, to dedicate your life to God, to experience the sacredness of the purpose you now take on, to receive your assignment, and to accept initiation into the brother-sisterhood of all the beings of light who serve the One.

THE INITIATION MEDITATION

Sit comfortably with your back erect. Close your eyes. Take a deep breath and sigh it out slowly. Now feel your whole body relaxing more and more with every breath that you take.

"Peace, be still. Peace, be still." Feel a flow of peace settling over your being. All the emotions of outer life depart, leaving only the deep, nurturing peace of God. You rest in the arms of Spirit and feel a wonderful sense of well-being. For a moment now, abandon your outer self and dwell totally in the inner kingdom.

Let your mind rest upon the words: *I, if I be lifted up, will draw all humanity unto me . . . I, if I be lifted up, will draw all humanity unto me.* Affirm the words silently: *I, if I be lifted up, will draw all humanity unto me.*

Keep repeating the words within until your whole being seems to thrill to the higher meaning and higher purpose they embody. *I, if I be lifted up . . .* Feel Spirit drawing you into the heights, feel yourself ascending in consciousness far beyond the confines of your present earthly life.

. . . will draw all humanity unto me. Sense that as you rise, everyone rises. Feel all human beings everywhere sharing your resurrection into higher consciousness. Feel them all joyously lifting out of limitation. Feel grateful that you are irresistibly tied to everyone else in the world. We rise together. And others will rise beyond us using the footholds we gain.

I, if I be lifted up, will draw all humanity unto me. Feel the high purpose you aspire to. Feel your dedication to becoming a bridge . . . your dedication to fulfilling God's highest purposes for your life.

Now, in your mind's eye, let your quest take visual form. See yourself walking down a quiet, secluded walkway to the sacred inner Temple that lies within you. You know this is the place where you will come face-to-face with God and dedicate your life to the Divine.

As you approach the door, hesitate, contemplating the sacred step you are about to take. Center yourself in your spiritual commitment. Focus your whole being upon the experience before you and walk through the door into the Temple.

As you enter, you realize that there is a great gathering of Light beings in your honor. They fill the sanctuary. Before you lies the center aisle leading to the altar in the front, and focusing your attention upon it, slowly and ceremoniously you make your way forward until you stand beyond the gathered crowd and alone before the altar.

A silence that is dynamic and latent with power fills the room. You are in the presence of the Almighty—God, the One. That Presence floods you with emotions and energies that are beyond description. It is as if you stand isolated from all else, face-to-face with the indefinable Presence from which we draw our very life. You feel Divine Love enfolding you, Divine Light brilliantly swelling all around you, Infinite Power permeating the atmosphere.

In utter humility, you kneel before the altar and dedicate your whole life to God. Every aspect of it. "God, use me in whatever way You will. All that I am is Yours." Offer your life as a spiritual explorer. "I will become Your spiritual laboratory that my struggles may become the means by which humanity discovers a piece of our higher identity and rises more fully

into Thy presence. Fill me with the strength to serve Thy purposes in every event of my life. Help me to make a difference."

Now ask: "God, what would You have me do? What shall
I explore? What shall be my assignment?" With expectation,
open your mind to receive direction. Spend a few moments in
silence, receptive to God's inspiration.

Now ask God for inspiration as to how to pursue your
spiritual goals. How will you fulfill your task? Where will you
start? What research should you do? What practices will help
you break through this virgin territory? How will you live it
out in your life? Once again, take a few moments in silence to
receive God's divine inspiration.

Having received and taking that inspiration deep into
your heart, rise and turn to face the gathering of angels, celestial beings, avatars, and great beings of Light. At their head is
your teacher, Jesus Christ. Their attention is upon you, and
they seem to be welcoming you directly from their hearts. The
feeling of acceptance is overwhelming.

Joy rises in the room as you realize that you are joining the
spiritual hierarchy. A voice resounds within your own being:
"The Holy Spirit, moving through you, initiates you into the
ranks of the Inner Core. Enter the spiritual hierarchy as a disciple of Jesus Christ, dedicated to spiritual awakening."

After a moment you focus upon the doors at the entrance
to the sanctuary and begin your path by resolutely walking
down the aisle back into your outer life. With you, you take
all the energy from your encounter with the Divine, your
assignment, the inspirations that go along with it, and the
shared consciousness of Light that you now dip into with all
of those who gathered on your behalf.

Keep the feelings from your inner encounter but now

sense your body once again. Feel yourself in your physical life, in this physical room, yet subtly merged with the spiritual experience you have just completed.

Take a deep breath. Sigh it out. Then another. Take joy in the feeling of well-being within your body and optimism for your life. Say out loud or silently: "Thank You, God, for Your presence with me now and always. Amen."

Before you do anything else, take time to journal what you experienced, what assignment you received, and any inspirations as to how you will go about exploring in your designated area.

FOLLOW YOUR GUIDANCE

Your experience may not have been what you expected. You may have been quite sure what area you would be working in, only to have something else come up during the meditation. The key here is to follow any guidance received. That which came to you during the time when you were totally open and receptive to God's direction has precedence over anything you figured out for yourself beforehand.

Liz had concluded that she would be approaching the central goal, that of awakening her Christ Self. Yet, during the initiation meditation, she was told to pursue her art—something she'd laid aside for some time. Mystified, she took up her paintbrush once again and was amazed at the joy that surged through her being as creativity was released.

She went on to do some "spirit drawing," a practice she'd been inspired to pursue. Blindfolded, she would paint her feelings onto the canvas, then excitedly look to see what creations came out of her subconscious. Her artwork broke something loose within her that had clogged the flow. In the process, it had moved her much farther down the road toward awakening her Christ Self.

Tom was certain he would be opening his heart as a project. He emerged from meditation saying he had received something, but he wasn't sure he liked it. "All I got was, 'Work on silence.' What does that mean? Is God telling me to be quiet?"

"Yes," I answered, "but this is a high and wonderful assignment. Inner silence is where all the exciting stuff of Spirit happens." Silence became for Tom his door into the heart. Anyone who has pursued silence has discovered that it leads to all the higher realms.

Once again, the assignment God gave him was truly a divine appointment.

What about the few of you who have returned from the initiation meditation with a wonderful experience but still no clarity on your assignment? Don't fret or resign to failure. Some people take longer to receive their instructions. As long as you felt the commitment, you are already on your way.

Observe your life over the next few days and see if something comes into focus that Spirit seems to be showing you. Sometimes the inspiration comes in a delayed reaction. If after a week nothing comes, make the best decision you can on your own. Occasionally we are asked to make up our own minds with God interfering only if we head in a destructive direction.

If you find yourself in this position, read over the list of suggested frontiers in the next chapter. Pay attention to anything that seems to "catch hold of you" when you do. Watch to see if something jumps out at you. It might be an area that seems particularly exciting. Or it could be a subject that causes you distress, as if it were a lesson that lay ahead, but you are resisting.

One individual stated: "I got a lot of energy off the section on purification. I felt my body get hot and an uneasy energy rise in me when you were talking about it. It isn't a subject I'm comfortable with, but I feel that's where my life is leading me."

Add all of your logic, inspiration, and contemplations together and come to some conclusions. Then take these results into meditation, seeking confirmation. If you realize that God is active in your mind, you can't really make a mistake. You do need to make a decision.

If after all of this you are still running in circles trying to decide what to explore, remember my suggestion to take the assignment of opening your heart. You will be following Jesus' instructions, and a little heart work should clear the way to perceive future assignments.

CHANGING DIRECTION

This brings up one last point. You may not stick with this one assignment. Down the road at any time, you may sense that you are finished for now and choose a new direction of exploration.

This is the natural flow of things, but it carries with it a pitfall. There are so many wonderful spiritual energies beckoning to us. There is a temptation to switch from project to project when one gets a little bored. If you never make it through the dreary stage in developing a certain quality, you never gain the prize.

Remember, I spent between five and seven years with heart as my main focus before sensing it was time to move on.

You won't do this with everything, but you will do it with a few projects.

When you accept an assignment, you won't give up all the other areas of spiritual learning. Life will continue to give you a well-balanced course of study. You simply choose to give emphasis to the spiritual exploration you have accepted, while giving only normal attention to all the other lessons demanded of you.

Keep in mind the words of one meditation teacher who stated: "When you dig a well, you don't find water by digging three feet down in a hundred places. You must dig a hundred feet down in one place."

Chapter 2

THE FRONTIERS

"There are no more frontiers!" one friend complained to another. Both had been intrigued by stories of bold, independent people from past generations who had gone into the wilderness, homesteaded land, and carved their corner of the Earth into something of real value, far from the confines of civilization.

In that day and age, one could always "go West." What about Daniel Boone? Legend says he kept moving west every time he could see his neighbor's chimney smoke. What an exciting challenge to pioneer new land . . . to be the foundation of a new world in the making.

The conversation continued: "Here we are, aspiring pioneers with no wilderness left to pit ourselves against. Antarctica is the only truly uninhabited continent, and without a polar shift to melt the ice, it will have to remain that way. Past generations had the New World, even Africa and Indonesia. The future will have space travel. I guess we are just in between with no frontiers available to us."

So often, the very thing we desire lies right in front of us, yet we don't recognize it because it takes a different form than we expect. Disappointed would-be pioneers need only lift their sights a little to find pristine, unexplored continents awaiting *within themselves.*

The future will look back on this generation as an exciting time when a bold, independent few broke through the barriers and explored inner realms of heart, mind, and Spirit, creating whole new lives that would change the very shape of civilization. They will yearn, "Oh, to have been one of those early pioneers, developing the very energies that are the foundation of life as we know it today."

No frontiers! Nothing could be farther from the truth. This is the most exciting time humankind has ever experienced on this planet. Frontiers are everywhere, and finally, we can see them.

For those who aren't entirely clear what spiritual frontiers need to be explored, I'm going to outline a short tour of a few that I can see. The list will obviously be incomplete and objectives rather cursory, but maybe the tour will get you thinking. Sometimes I might mention an unfamiliar term or practice, but your looking it up is part of your exploration.

Some areas will hit you as being rather secular, while others will seem quite sacred. Who knows what piece of consciousness development you will recognize as your assignment. You might find something here that sparks a resonance in your soul. Or you may hear something calling to you that lies beyond the areas mentioned.

Opening the Heart: I mention this first because, from personal experience, I know the possibilities available to you through this door are unlimited. Concentrate on your heart, and you will break through to realms of feeling and knowing that allow you to see far beyond the confines of mental processes, to place power behind thoughts and prayers, to encounter spiritual experience directly rather than constantly feel removed from it. Whatever you are doing, try to do it with your heart and you will see big changes in your results. The heart is an exciting ride to almost anywhere within the spiritual realms.

Healing: Healing has always been one of the spiritual frontiers. It still is. Research here may include some of the multitude of healing techniques, learning the tools until you can achieve consistent results. Yet I hope some of you will reach beyond the tools to isolate the basic healing Life Force that does all healing no matter what technique is employed. This is the energy the woman experienced who was healed by touching the hem of Jesus' robe (metaphysically meaning his consciousness) as he passed. The ultimate healing excursion would be to incorporate this energy so strongly into your consciousness that others could become aware of this energy in themselves just by encountering it in you.

Guidance and Intuition: Divine Mind already has every answer you could ever want. How can we tap in? Explore how guidance comes to you. Learn to distinguish that still, small (accurate) voice from the clamoring personality voices that surround it. Devise all manner of ways to consult guidance and then check out whether it is right or wrong. I once set about using investments as an experiment in guidance. I could always check my results in the paper the next day. I learned a pendulum wouldn't work for me. Neither would applied kinesiology. I learned there is a quiet inner knowing that is always right, and the voices of greed or fear, which feel a little different, are always wrong. I learned you must develop a love for what you want to know. When you make the important decisions of life, you need to know wisdom is showing you your way.

Christ Qualities: Everything you have ever wanted or needed in this life can be related back to a basic, primal spiritual energy available within yourself. Love, abundance, life, peace, joy, beauty . . . these are what we really seek. The outer things are all designed to give us one of these energies. But they are really available only from within. We hope the outer attainment will spark the inner energy. I call the inner energies *Christ qualities.* Why not short-circuit the process and generate them within yourself without need of an outer stimulus? Choose a quality. Meditate on it. Affirm it. Concentrate on it throughout your day until it becomes a natural part of your consciousness. Then see how your outer life has shifted to reflect what you are naturally generating.

Self-Esteem Building: To truly become a Christ being, you are first going to have to build a consciousness that believes it is worthy of being a higher Self. Explore ways to feel your inner majesty as a child of God while you walk through life. Along the way, you will have to learn to distinguish between self-esteem with a small "s" and Self-esteem with a large "S." Future generations will grow up in these patterns of high Self-esteem.

Jesus' Footsteps: Can you immerse yourself in the consciousness of Jesus Christ? Affirm and meditate on his presence until you can feel a deep kinship with it and know that Jesus is your teacher and you, his disciple. Work on this intensely enough and you may have an encounter that will dramatically change your life. Contemplate what it would be like to be the man who said: "The Father and I are one" (RSV), "I am the light of the world," "Whoever has seen me has seen the Father" (RSV), "I am the way, and the truth, and the life" (RSV), "I, if I be lifted up from the earth, will draw all men unto me."

Use Jesus' power statements until you can sense what it felt like to carry his consciousness through physical life. Imitation of the Master is the oldest path to enlightenment.

Silence: Mastering silence is one of the most important expeditions on the spiritual path. Much of higher perception is communicated in silence. Start by getting comfortable with silence. Sit silently with someone and enjoy a sunset. Feel the silent bond that exists with nature. Learn to enjoy aloneness. Use silence to generate energy behind your words or actions. And of course, meditate, striving to reach the silence. You may want to employ the spiritual practice of retreat, arranging to be completely alone for an extended period without escapes like TV, radio, or books. One cannot comprehend the strength that comes from spending several days, weeks, or even months in silent retreat.

Mastering Abundance: It is one thing to apply prosperity techniques to get what you want and entirely another to sculpt a consciousness of abundance that naturally surrounds you and to have that energy flowing so strongly that those you come in contact with automatically wake up to abundance within themselves. There's plenty of material and practices out there. Just remember it is not an outer result you are looking for. That is a by-product. You are looking for a divine energy and ways to sew it into your everyday garment of consciousness. If I could put a name on this energy, I would call it *gratefulness.* A shortcut is to build as much gratefulness into your daily life as possible.

Imagination: Tapping the power of imagination can be as much fun as work. This path investigates creating with our imaging faculty. It may start with a "treasure map" of pictures of the things you want to demonstrate in life or daily imagery of that car you want to own, but the frontier runs much deeper. Here we learn that reality is not static, but in motion and that we can alter the picture by participating in the drawing process. Learning to bend reality in all manner of directions through constant use of our imaginative faculty will change the whole way humanity perceives life. You may have to begin by bringing into awareness the ways we are already participating in this creative process and how one accepts or rejects the gathered images of past generations still latent in the human-race mind.

Creativity: This is the process by which one plugs low-voltage human mind into high voltage from the higher realms and turns out art, music, ideas, writings, inventions, problem-solving techniques, and on and on, all of which may seem far beyond his or her seeming capabilities. Creativity involves a quantum leap to higher functioning of mind. We need creativity to survive and be happy. Experiment with different ways to plug in. What is required to make the connection? How does the higher voltage feel in your body? How can you learn to trust it more? Can you devise techniques for bypassing human limits and touching creativity directly? An artist's example is painting your feelings with your eyes blindfolded to see what images take form. In each area, learning to let go and to let the energy flow is essential. Humanity thirsts for creativity, in any of its forms.

Mastering Personality: At this stage in human evolution, our personalities are in charge. In the future, the Higher Being, the Christ Self, will be master of his or her personality. Many of the personal challenges we face set up a course of study whereby we could learn to take control of ourselves rather than letting personality run wild like a spoiled child. The strength gained from the struggle is necessary for one to function as the Christ Self. Emotional mastery is the first hurdle, learning to switch emotional states on cue for the greater benefit of the being, then generating whatever emotion we choose. More advanced lessons include accepting the unacceptable. The common spiritual student avoids taking responsibility for his or her every personal reaction, desire, decision, or pattern. The frontier lies in becoming master of oneself, and everyday life provides the perfect testing ground.

Purification: This carries the last concept a little further in a specific direction. The path of purification rests upon the realization that the amount of light shining through a dirty kerosene lamp increases relative to the amount of black soot one cleans from the globe. Illumination is achieved by wiping away all the dirt. The pioneer in this area pours intense effort into clearing all personal negativity, vulgarity, fear, anger, resentment, and selfish desire. One watches his or her words, thoughts, feelings, and actions with the intention of creating a clear vessel for Spirit to use. A simple, healthy diet and body habits become the outer symbol of inner cleansing work. One might pursue contemplation of past experiences that still have negative emotional reactions connected to them. Go through your life and relive a past experience from your present consciousness, changing it, and remembering you are not still that same person. You have evolved. You need not carry it further. Purify yourself. Simplify your life. Then observe how your light seems to shine more clearly.

Light: Working with light directly opens amazing doors. Meditate on light. Imagine yourself glowing in light until it is no longer an image you hold. You actually are aware that you are glowing in light. Then observe how the world around you seems to change after a session in the light. If you can't see light, then concentrate on the color white until it comes easier. Start sending light to people. Anytime something needs protection, surround it in light. Lower a shield of light around you each morning that will reflect all harm while allowing everything else to flow through freely. Light has always been symbolic of God—all that is good. When you concentrate on light, you awaken awareness of God—or Light. In the end, we are beings of Light. It is a powerful area to develop.

The Holy Spirit: The Holy Spirit is God in action, the Spirit that sets up the whole learning program of life. In this area of exploration, we strive to set up a firm connection with the Holy Spirit and work with It directly. This is the Spirit that Jesus said he would send to teach us all we need to know. Begin by affirming the Holy Spirit active in your life. Begin looking at each experience as something set up for you by the Holy Spirit. Commit to serving Spirit. Meditate on the rush of the wind that is often described along with the flow of the Holy Spirit. Develop your own ways to touch Spirit. A real connection forged here should produce major observable results.

Christ Self: For those who want to "go for the gold," set your sights firmly on becoming your Christ Self. This is following in Jesus' footsteps to the fullest. This mountain seems off in the distance through an unexplored wilderness. Start by affirming: *I am the Christ, the son/daughter of God!* Keep at it until the words lose their emptiness and start to resonate within you. Realize that a higher Self exists within you and start trying to communicate with it. Set up a working relationship with your higher Self, trusting it to do the real work while your outer self does the best it can or simply entertains.

Finally, start the process of merging with this awe-inspiring Being within.

Nature: For many, communicating with nature is the perfect spiritual adventure. Explore the power of prayer on plants. As a gardener, I've seen roses do the seemingly impossible in order to cooperate with my desires, once I set up a deep relationship with them. Meditate on a tree until you understand "tree-ness." Communicate, heart-to-heart, with animals, or learn to hear their telepathy. Feel the spirit of the land you live on. Explore Native American approaches. I've seen the wind and animals from the wild respond in miraculous ways during Native American ceremonies. On your own, merge with the wind. Take the power of the storm into your being. Become one with the forces of nature until they seem to accept you, even cradle you, rather than tear against you.

Relationship Work: This laboratory has all the lessons necessary for the advanced being. Search for the spiritual connection that each relationship—mother, father, child, mate, family, friend—provides. Identify and realize the importance of your spiritual family. Discover the difference between your positive attractions and your negative attractions. Pursue couple's practices for spiritually attuning yourself to someone else. Master silent consciousness encounters and the spiritual energies exchanged. Make them conscious, thus taking responsibility for a higher outcome. Through experience, we learn the higher spiritual laws of relationship. Future generations will need to learn them early in order not to get bogged down.

Oneness: It sounds easy enough. Many claim to have explored it but few really have. "I love the whole world. It's just the people I can't stand," does not qualify. Truly absorbing that everyone and everything is part of me is a large assignment.

Becoming part of the whole is where it begins, but the jump to oneness consciousness from individual consciousness is a big one. Reach for direct communication with "the One." Stretch yourself very high to an intelligence that intimately knows and loves everything in the universe and countless dimensions beyond, while we struggle to keep our little lives in order. Imagine a thought trying to communicate with the mind as a whole.

Youth Consciousness: I know of individuals banded together to uncover spiritual principles for extending healthy life in the body. They are exploring nutrients, lifestyles, stress control, exercise and, most important, thought patterns, emotional patterns, meditation exercises, and spiritual principles for keeping our bodies young and extending our lives. Future generations will do this. Possibly, you'd like to help break ground now.

Divine Power: Have you ever stood on that high ground where for a few moments you knew that if you told the mountain to move, it would move because you (and everyone else) were connected directly to Divine Power? Getting to that space is a warrior's journey. What is required to merge with the power of God and perform seeming miracles? If you set your sights on this task, you will learn to step aside and let something else do the work through you. You will discover that Divine Power uses us. We don't use it. You will excitedly explore a realm where earthly limits don't mean a thing. To have full access to power and use it only as God directs is an art that requires its own brand of intense self-discipline.

Spiritual Business Principles: Can you imagine a business world run strictly on spiritual principles? It begins with a few willing to commit their lives to proving that a business run by spiritual law will prosper more than the best one run by dog-eat-dog business rules. When God is your partner, certain practices are off-limits. However, higher unseen forces come to your assistance. This will have to be proven with physical evidence. Step-by-step guidance will have to be recorded to show exactly how one goes about setting up this business relationship with the Divine. This work will transform the face of the marketplace.

Dream Work: This is one of those exciting areas that capture the imagination. It is a whole other world that we haphazardly enter each night. Master it and your life seems to double. Learn to remember your dreams, to dream true, and to see the symbolism. Isolate the feelings and preparations that invite prophetic dreaming. Strive for increased frequency and accuracy. Study how you can learn something in the dream state and carry the lessons into your outer life too. The real fun begins when you enter into lucid dreaming. You realize you are dreaming and take the reins. There are places to go, new realms to explore. This work comes full circle when you realize that Earth life is nothing more than a solidified dream state. If you can loosen your grip on reality, you can change your outer life in exactly the same way you direct your dreams.

Letting Go: Begin by learning the difference between releasing and submerging. There is an art to letting go and an illusive energy state always present when release truly takes place. Letting go is its own path into the Divine. Let go of everything you hang on to for support, one by one. Fear will challenge you every step of the way. At the far end of this path, you will come to a cliff. Walk to the edge. Fear will try to drive you back. Don't let it. Jump. Abandon yourself into the unknown of God. Then come back and tell us how to follow. Tell us how it changed your life.

Meditation Journeys: There are thousands of meditation techniques taking one to millions of spiritual states. Explore as many as you can. Determine which ones create the most unusual and dramatic results for you. Then teach others how to get there faster than you did. Have you ever spent four hours a day in meditation on an extended basis? Those who have can share the dramatic results their lives produced.

Color: We are just now doing serious groundbreaking on the spiritual stimulation that color has in our lives. Schools are using color therapy in their classrooms. Meditate on red or green, yellow or blue. Feel the different energies these colors channel into your being. Using stained glass or colored light-bulbs, experiment with the energies you feel in your body when bathed in different colored lights. Then devise ways to apply the information you've gleaned to outer life.

Sound and Music: What is the spiritual impact of sound or music? Both have been used throughout the ages to encourage spiritual experience. Musicians can create music to inspire certain states of consciousness. Music lovers can experiment with recorded music in meditation. Sound itself vibrates spiritual energy centers. Sound can heal, break up areas of consciousness where we are blocked. The spiritual science of sound is ancient, yet relatively undeveloped in the modern sense.

Spiritual Energy Centers: Concentration on the seven chakras or the physical locations for the twelve powers will catapult you forward. It's like doing a body workout. You can't relate anything directly to the exercises you do every day, but the regimen changes the whole way you feel about life, your energy level, and thus, everything you do. A spiritual workout on the energy centers strengthens your consciousness and, thus, your whole spiritual life. Things start to happen that you weren't strong enough to experience before. Sound, affirmation, light, and concentration are excellent tools to start the work on these centers.

Regeneration: This is the development of the spiritual body and the slow but sure transfer of your body reality from the physical to this higher level. Energy-center concentration is a contribution to this realm. However, the process is much more universal. Every time you make an affirmation, pray, depend on guidance, or reach out with your heart to touch someone, you are embodying yourself more clearly within your spiritual body. We need to bring the process out of unconsciousness. We need to see the transfer of body identity taking place. The field is wide open if you want to take it on.

Breathwork: Breathing techniques have been a part of the spiritual path for thousands of years. After all, the breath is an excellent physical rheostat for changing consciousness. There are countless studies in different types of breathwork. Learn to slow the breath and experience the changes. At one point, I learned to breathe fifteen full, deep breaths in fifteen minutes. The change in consciousness was dramatic. Different types of breathing (for example, in through the nose and out through the mouth, or in through the nose and out through the nose) create different types of spiritual energy within the being. Then we have the deep, rapid, continuous breath that can bring on emotional cleansing or stimulate advanced spiritual experience. Once again the instructions are to experiment, master, and teach.

Body Mastery: It's like training a horse. A disciplined body can serve you well on this spiritual journey. At our present stage of human development, the body is still in charge. We need to master the body and put the intangible being in charge. Place your body in training. Work with diet or fasting. Teach it to be hot or cold on command. Take control of your heart so you can slow it at will. Use spiritual practices to create instant strength or instill health. Practice with any unusual body capability you choose until you master it. The body of the future will respond to the driver like a sports car, not the "clunker" most of us drive around in today.

Spiritual Sexuality: It's time to take sexual activity out of the physical closet and recognize it as the spiritual experience it was always meant to be. Surprisingly enough, this can start with an excursion into celibacy. Nothing can teach you more about the nonphysical side of sexuality than removing its physical counterpart. Study and isolate nonphysical sexual exchanges. They are subtle, but once highlighted, they can become fulfilling. Concentrate on your bottom chakra until sexual energy is released. Then learn to lift it by observing it, yet not allowing it to flow sexually. When you add the physical and nonphysical back together, explore some tantra techniques. Create your own techniques for merging spiritually and not being swept away by the physical and emotional passions.

Advanced Mind Powers: Here one might choose a partner and set up experiments in telepathy. Maybe you will pursue astral projection, the ability to leave your body and go somewhere else to observe or, in advanced stages, communicate with another. Experiment in psychometry, holding a physical object and sensing its owner or the experiences it has been through. You could start just by taking the time to feel the vibrations around you in life wherever you go and learning to use that information. Yes, these are mind games, instead of the deeper experience of connecting with God. But awakened children of God will use all of these faculties without giving them much thought. As long as we keep them in perspective, it wouldn't hurt to start introducing humanity to them.

Using Thought Forms: Certain images have always been used to convey a spiritual energy or experience: sending a good dragon for protection or a unicorn to bring abundance, imagining Cupid creating romance, using thought forms in prayers. The pictures are nothing more than that—pictures. But when we concentrate on them with enough energy, we breathe life into them. Our ideas are our creations. That is how we are created in the image of God. The thought form thus created admirably acts as a container for the spiritual energy we pour into it. We do this unconsciously already. Learning to consciously and constructively use thought forms may seem gimmicky, but it's a nice middle-ground step for those traveling from physical security to spiritual security. A number of mind-training groups already use it extensively with excellent results.

Mind Over Matter: Dissolving clouds, walking on hot coals, levitating, stilling the storm, and moving objects through telekinesis—all are exercises in mind over matter that different individuals are working with today. This falls into the realm of seeking after phenomena, but why not? One's gut-level outlook on life changes dramatically the first time he or she participates in breaking physical laws. Once again, future generations will take this as a matter of course. Someone must start the process now.

Efficient Mental Processes: Memory techniques, triggering mechanisms, efficiency states of mind—all increase our effectiveness in our human lives. The mental machinery needs to be trained and refined just as the body needs to be.

Shamanic Spiritual Experience: The aboriginal and native cultures of the world all have their own mechanisms for navigating the spiritual path. It can be an interesting experience to study them and travel a little of their ground. In the end, they can shed light on the paths we walk because their spirituality is based on experience, not philosophy.

Soul Memory: If past-life memory is important to you, you may want to explore some of the meditation techniques for going back. "Running," "time tracking," "soul travel"—all are names of processes that can bring other life memory. Use what information you gain to make this life better or else the exploration is useless. In the end, it doesn't matter what eternity model you use—reincarnation, heaven and hell, or progression through other dimensions. All that matters is what you do with "now." These models are designed for human understanding of something too vast for the human mind to grasp. Go back with purpose, not just for entertainment. And don't get lost in going back or you will be sidetracked from your *now* experience.

Angels, Fairies, and Divas: God's blessings are conveyed to the physical world by a variety of paths. People have seen angels for thousands of years and experienced miracles in their presence. Just as one can speak to the higher Self of a human being, we can surely communicate with the archetype or diva of the common garden pea. And those vortexes of energy that seem to be constantly nurturing the many forms nature takes, could they be fairies? I have close friends who have banded together to share their angel encounters and explore how we can encourage this type of contact with these higher energy expressions of God. Will the future open the doors between human expression and angelic expression, enabling us to work together fully?

Spiritual Technology: This is the perfect crossover for the engineers in our midst. Science is developing machinery to aid us in our journeys through consciousness. Brain wave measurement, biofeedback, the brain wave synchronizer, binaural wave generation and tapes, certain waves sent through the brain, electrical currents sent through nerve centers, and virtual reality meditation equipment are just the beginning. Someone needs to explore them all and determine what is truly helpful and what is not as well as what spiritual phenomenon is actually being produced in each instance.

Communicating With the Earth: Everything in the universe is alive. The planets and stars are not just dead rocks and fiery infernos. They are higher orders of life that lie almost beyond our comprehension. However, as children of the Earth, we can stretch out and touch the being we feed from in much the same way we stretch out to try to embrace the "oneness" of God.

Conclusions: This list of the frontiers is incomplete. In fact, it only scratches the surface. Some of the examples deal with deep core issues of the spiritual path and some deal with phenomena. Advanced beings will incorporate and use both in their daily lives.

The frontiers that include phenomena will include a lot of fantasy for most of us at this stage in our development. Spiritual explorers must learn to separate fantasy from expanded spiritual reality and then demonstrate how to create this experience in their lives.

I hope on the way through the list of frontiers that you got inspired. Maybe some area seemed to resonate within you or captured your imagination. Possibly you jumped to an idea that wasn't mentioned. In either case, I hope you started to get a feel for what area you are drawn to. You can't do it all. Shortly, you will have to make a choice as to what adventure to embark upon. Can you sense what frontier is calling to you?

Chapter 3

RESEARCH

When I was in my mid-twenties, a friend and I decided we would like to pursue furniture upholstering as a hobby. My friend immediately informed me that we were in luck because there was a class on furniture upholstering at the local community college. It would begin in three weeks, and we should sign up.

I had other ideas. I wanted to start now. So I went to the local library, found a how-to book on upholstering, read it, and studied the techniques. Then I went to the local thrift shop, bought myself an old, worn $4 chair, and plowed into learning by experience. I had my new, brown velour masterpiece finished before my friend got word that his class was cancelled for that quarter.

You will probably have to fulfill your spiritual exploration in much the same way I approached upholstering. You'll learn your most valuable lessons on your own. But to start with, you will want to do a little research.

There may be classes available that apply to the area you intend to pursue. Treat these classes as background work. Earthbound teachers do their best, but none of them have all the answers. There's always a lot left for the pioneer to explore.

Use workshops and classes as an opportunity to familiarize yourself with current levels of attainment in your chosen area of study. They are not the answer to your quest, merely a jumping-off point, if you so choose.

You may come upon some valuable information just by asking friends, spiritual leaders, or your spiritual partners what kinds of experiences they have had in your assigned category. If you get a response, ask them what they did to facilitate the experience or what state of consciousness accompanied it.

Don't ask what they think about the subject or you will never get to the good stuff. Philosophy will devour your conversation. Gather ideas of what to do, filter out what you can use, and plan how you will embark on your journey.

There are movies and tapes that may hold just the jewel you are looking for, but books are the most obvious resources you have at your disposal. Here, like everywhere else, you must use discrimination.

There are numerous books on almost every subject, but only a few will be valuable to you. Books that merely philosophize are very nearly useless. Books skillfully written by someone who has acted like a news reporter on the scene of those having spiritual experience may be a better bet. Yet, in the end, these can fall short too. You want to read books written by someone who has actually walked where you hope to travel. Why read about the mystics or their philosophy when you can read the mystics' own account of their journey? Let those explorers who have gone before you tell you personally of their experience.

Individuals like Charles and Myrtle Fillmore, Ernest Holmes, Emma Curtis Hopkins, and Mary Baker Eddy are just a handful of modern explorers who actually walked the paths they reported. Their books outline the results of their inner research and the vision of life they gained. In the midst of all of this, you will find the jewels you seek. These writers will periodically share the experiences that led them to their realization. They leave just enough of a clue as to how they got there that a focused spiritual explorer can follow and find a similar experience.

There are hundreds of other names that could be added to the list. Some are farther back in history. Others are even more current than those just listed. What ties them all together is this: They had their own experiences. They didn't just report what someone else did. Yet it is easy to miss the very aspect of their books that sets them above the multitude of spiritual writings around them.

PRACTICE WHAT YOU READ

Many years ago a partner on the path, Jim, reported to me that *Lessons in Truth* by H. Emilie Cady had changed his life. An acquaintance had given it to him. It sat in the glove compartment of his car for months because Jim thought the man had insulted him by giving him a book on how to be truthful. It literally fell into his lap during one of the low points of his life, and he started to read.

Each chapter carried advice he desperately needed. As he worked his way through the book, his spirits climbed from the pits to the heights. He was launched on a voyage that has never ended.

Jim told me: "It took me quite a while to get through the whole book because I stopped and did whatever it said to do. If Cady said to repeat an affirmation or a scripture over and over, I laid the book down and spent time affirming. If she said to meditate on a certain idea or pray in a certain way, I stopped to meditate or to pray. If she said to do something in your life, I went out and did it." He went on to describe the specific things he'd done under the book's direction.

I couldn't remember most of these little tasks, though I'd read *Lessons in Truth.* I read it straight through a few chapters at a time. I enjoyed the book very much. I thought it to be an excellent primer on spiritual principles, but it didn't change my life. I determined the difference in impact lay in the way we each had chosen to read the book.

Years later I learned the lesson again, but at a deeper level of intensity. As a dedicated student of the writings of Charles and Myrtle Fillmore, I had read all of their published books a number of times. I had taught classes on each and could quote verbatim all my favorite passages. I loved the perspective of life they painted and gave this research credit for carrying me far down my own spiritual path.

At the urging of some close friends, I started attending the functions of a mystical spiritual order from another philosophy. At first, I went kicking and screaming because it all felt so alien to me. But shortly, I began to see some advantages to the way they did things.

This group stressed a thing called *practices,* which is a specific activity meant to create an atmosphere which would invite a spiritual experience. I constantly chafed at the bit when encountering secrecy and rituals for the sake of ritual. I disliked the totally sober attitude taken toward spirituality and the political ranks that disciples attained. Though an initiate for six years, I never really belonged to this group consciousness, yet I learned a lot, and this trip expanded my spiritual horizons immensely.

I repeated short prayer statements in foreign languages over and over, first aloud, then silently. I worked with sound, body motions, and all manner of inner-energy exercises. I learned the meaning of discipleship and contemplated different aspects of God. I learned new ways of meditating on Light and gleaned ways of awakening spiritual energy centers.

I was constantly adapting what I learned to my basic vision of life and my spiritual tradition. I developed prayer statements with English words which embodied the same sounds that were so important in the foreign ones. I altered many of the practices to fit into the meditation structures already in use by other students of the Fillmores. I discarded anything that conflicted with the basic Truth structure I had absorbed and used everything else to shed greater light on these principles.

After a time my understanding and expression of spiritual realities expanded so dramatically that I began to question why the Fillmore writings hadn't conveyed something like these practices I'd discovered and adapted. I picked up the Fillmore books I'd taught so many times and reread them, looking for some sign that the spiritual explorers, whose thoughts had guided my path thus far, had seen some of the things I'd found.

Like magic, practices jumped out at me from every chapter, as if they'd been hiding behind bushes. Pages that I thought I knew by heart sprouted suggestions I'd never seen before. Everything I'd foraged in the "far country" was available right here at home. You just had to know how to read. You had to approach the material as a spiritual explorer, not a philosopher. A spiritual explorer will find that the vast majority of mystics have seen much of the same territory, even if their perspective and emphasis are different.

READ AS A SPIRITUAL EXPLORER

The technique for researching practices or perceptions that can be used to create practices is universal. It works for all authors, all books. Since the Fillmores' writings have been my emphasis, let me use them to demonstrate what to look for.

Myrtle Fillmore's healing of terminal tuberculosis was the beginning of everything for the Fillmores. Much has been written on realizations in the area of healing, but in *How to Let God Help You* in the chapter entitled "Health in the Home" (pp. 125–126), Myrtle tells of the practices by which she pursued healing:

Here is the key to my discovery. Life has to be guided by intelligence in making all forms. The same law works in my own body. Life is simply a form of energy and has to be guided and directed in man's body by his intelligence. How do we communicate intelligence? By thinking and talking, of course. Then it flashed upon me that I might talk to the life in every part of my body and have it do just what I wanted. I began to teach my body and got marvelous results.

I told the life in my liver that it was not torpid or inert, but full of vigor and energy. I told the life in my stomach that it was not weak or inefficient, but energetic, strong, and intelligent. I told the life in my abdomen that it was no longer infested with ignorant ideas of disease, put there by myself and by doctors, but it was all athrill with the sweet, pure, wholesome energy of God. I told my limbs that they were active and strong. I told my eyes that they did not see of themselves but that they expressed the sight of Spirit and that they were drawing on an unlimited source. I told them that they were young eyes, clear, bright eyes, because the light of God shone right through them. I told my heart that the pure love of Jesus Christ flowed in and out through its beatings and that all the world felt its joyous pulsation.

I went to all the life centers of my body and spoke words of Truth to them—words of strength and power. I asked their forgiveness for the foolish, ignorant course that I had pursued in the past, when I condemned them and called them weak, inefficient, and diseased. I did not become discouraged at their being slow to wake up, but kept right on, both silently and aloud, declaring the words of Truth, until the organs responded.

How could she have been more clear? I've referred countless people inquiring about healing to these three paragraphs. To obtain the treasure they hold, you must leave behind the attitude, Isn't it wonderful that she was able to do this! and embrace, I want to do that too. I'm going to try this out and stick with it until I get results in my own body.

Start talking to your body. Change the words as you like. Affirm out loud. Silently. Then try singing the message, writing it—any variation you can think of. See yourself communicating with every cell. Visualize cells, organs, muscles, and bones responding. Take note of her admonition not to give up just because of slow response by the body. She's talking about real-life experience here: the intent, the process, and the obstacles. This is something you can do, not just think about.

OPENING THE HEART

Charles Fillmore addressed the opening of the heart in *Talks on Truth* within the chapter entitled "The Development of Divine Love" (pp. 62, 63):

We have been taught the beauties of love and its great power in the world, but no one else has explained that it has a center of action in the body, a center that was designed by the Creator to do a specific work. The man or the woman who has not developed the love center is abnormal, is living in only partial exercise of consciousness . . .

To develop the love center, begin by affirming: *From this time forth and forevermore I shall know no man after the flesh. I shall not see men and women as body and mortal thought. I shall always behold them with the eye of love, which sees only perfection.* Ask daily that love be made alive in you, that it take up its abode at your magnetic center, and make it alive with strong, steady pulsations of spiritual energy.

Let your attention rest for a few moments every day at the heart center in your body, the cardiac plexus, while you declare silently: *You are the abode of love. You are filled and thrilled with the mighty magnetic forces that love uses in doing its work. You are powerful and active to do only good, and you see only goodness and purity everywhere.*

I'm not fond of long affirmations. It takes too much intellectual energy to remember them, and I want to get beyond the intellect. But Fillmore clearly suggests to locate your cardiac plexus, your heart center, and start affirming that it is open. Create your own affirmation or use a piece of his. Use all of it if you like. Affirm pure love, Divine Love, flowing through this center, and keep affirming until you feel something happen. He suggests that you pray, asking God to open your heart center and desire to feel that divine flow.

Taking the words of Fillmore's first affirmation about seeing all men and women with spiritual eyes of love and seeing their perfection, we have a practice that can be adapted to daily life. Attempt to see each person you meet through eyes of love.

Finally, in meditation, visualize "strong, steady pulsations of spiritual energy" surging through your heart center. I have adapted this to affirming aloud the statement *Feel love!* while dropping my head as if driving a shaft of Light from my third eye center into my heart center. Then I slowly lift my head, rising on the energy released from the heart and begin the cycle again. When used over and over, this has been very effective in awakening heart energy. All of this provides a wealth of practices for exploring into the heart.

ENTERING SILENCE

In *Teach Us to Pray* (pp. 18, 24), Fillmore teaches the practice for entering Silence:

> By quieting the mental man, by passing through the discipline of intellectual silence, man arrives at the very threshold of God's workshop, the threshold of Being. . . .
>
> When entering the silence, according to Hosea, the command is "take with you words, and return unto Jehovah." After many centuries this instruction still stands approved today. To the metaphysician it means to close the eyes and ears to the without, to go within and hold the mind steadily on the word *Jehovah* until that word illumines the whole inner consciousness. Then, affirm a prayer such as *Thy vitalizing energy floods my whole consciousness, and I am healed.*
>
> Think what the mighty vitalizing energy of God, released through Jesus Christ, really is. Penetrate deeper into God consciousness within you and hold the prayer steadily until you attain spiritual realization . . . .

Here Fillmore has outlined the basic practice of entering the Silence. First, quiet the mind in intellectual silence. Then, realize that what you seek lies beyond in a realm that is dynamic and alive but not intellectual. Center your mind on God, concentrate on an affirmation, meditate upon its deeper meaning and finally, break through to realization in a realm where the intellect is silent and the heart experiences the dynamic activity of God.

STARTING CHAKRA WORK

In *Atom-Smashing Power of Mind* (p. 24), Charles tells how he started chakra work:

> It began when I was mentally affirming statements of Truth. Just between my eyes, but above, I felt a "thrill" that lasted a few moments, then passed away. I found I could repeat this experience with affirmations. As time went on I could set up this "thrill" at other points in my body and finally it became a continuous current throughout my nervous system. I called it "the Spirit" and found that it was connected with a universal life force whose source was the Christ.

An adaptation of this might be to affirm something like *I see clearly!* while concentrating on your third eye center. Do it until you feel the energy response. Then you could set about using affirmations at the other energy centers. Fillmore did and obviously got results. You could also begin to work with the descending and ascending currents of energy described by Cora Fillmore in "Christ Enthroned in Man" (*The Twelve Powers,* pp. 212–213).

It is Fillmore who first suggested using Jesus' power statements over and over like a mantra until they penetrate your consciousness in a way that is beyond words.

In *Talks on Truth* (p. 177), he writes: "Have you kept the sayings of Jesus? Have you said to yourself in silence and aloud until the very ethers vibrated with its Truth, 'I and the Father are one'?"

I've found that this type of practice can produce powerful results. Affirm Jesus' power statement over and over, striving to feel what it must be like to be the Master who could speak these words. Declare Jesus' statement aloud, then silently. Examine what effect this declaration has on your consciousness. What does it feel like to release the absurdity of your speaking these words and truly enter Jesus' consciousness? We don't understand what Fillmore was getting at until we immerse ourselves in the practice as he obviously did.

These examples of practices are obvious and easy to recognize. The Fillmore writings are full of them, especially affirmations to be used intensely to produce certain results. But not all reference to a practice is as straightforward. Sometimes we have to read between the lines.

PRACTICING RADIATING LIGHT

For instance, in *Atom-Smashing Power of Mind*, within the chapter entitled "Truth Radiates Light" (p. 81), Fillmore writes, "When the mind is lifted up in meditation and prayer, the whole body glows with spiritual light."

Ask yourself, "How does he know this?" The answer lies in the realization that to know this to be true, Fillmore must have experienced the radiance of this spiritual Light while praying. It must have been a real spiritual experience that another spiritual explorer could pursue. And for us, it remains philosophy

until we have stood on that same ground which enabled
Fillmore to declare this with the authority only experience
can give.

We could pray and meditate upon God, keeping an eye
out for a sense of spiritual Light. Or we could turn it back-
wards and meditate on glowing in light to see where that
would take us. It's kind of like working on a math problem
when you know the answer: the processes necessary to carry
you to the appropriate result come into focus much more
quickly.

Concentrate on the image of glowing in spiritual Light
while in meditation and you will eventually break through to
a higher realm where you experience yourself as a radiant
Light Being without holding to any image.

Fillmore refers to spiritual experience involving light in a
multitude of places, but in *Talks on Truth* (p. 152), he suggests:
"The live cells have a little electric light at their center, and the
dead ones are dark. In good health, there is a preponderance
of the light cells; in ill health the dark cells predominate.
Metaphysicians have found that man can light up the body
cells by affirming life and intelligence for them."

Fillmore goes on to recommend affirming "life" day and
night to create health. This is an excellent practice, but if you
are pursuing awareness of Light, you must do just that—put
it into *practice*. Knowing it as a philosophical ideal is not
enough. Take that image of light cells and dark cells, turn on
the light in the dark cells, and see what you can do with it.

In meditation, we could go to areas of the body that are
less than vibrant and concentrate on generating light in dark
cells. We could go further by meditating on God's celestial
light of life descending through the top of our head and slowly

moving downward through the whole body. As you work your way down, you will note that certain areas seem darker while other areas easily become radiant. Return to the dark areas and swirl the celestial Light through them until they finally begin to glow as brightly as the areas that readily light up. If you have trouble, imagine yourself going to the cellular level and instilling the spiritual Light one cell at a time until they all start to respond.

Every time you are captivated by an image or a concept that one of the mystics presents, realize that there is a spiritual experience which led to this revelation. You know the answer, so now it's time to explore paths which could lead to the experience that spawned it. Create practices that revolve around this particular image or concept. Use these practices as vehicles for exploring the area outlined.

Eventually, you will find yourself standing upon ground that gives you the same experiential revelation which the mystics relayed. In that moment, you will not just agree with what they said. You will know with certainty why they said it. You will have the revelation in the same way they did, as if you were the first ever to discover it.

Concepts come and go. They are fun to play with, but hard times can take a beautiful concept you claim to own and crash it on the rocks. Experiential revelation changes your life forever. Nothing can steal it from you.

Your research begins with the study of the mystics. It can only progress when you follow experientially in their footsteps and become a mystic yourself.

Chapter 4

TRAILBLAZING

A number of years ago a friend took me backpacking in the Sierra Nevada Mountains. We drove up to the trailhead, consulted our contour map, picked out the right colored trail marker, and started off on our two-day trek. We could check the map to see how far we'd gone, judging by the landmarks we crossed. We knew ahead of time what sights to look for. We had planned where we would camp and how many miles we would cover each day.

It was beautiful country, and my friend was much better at striding through the miles than I. Yet every time I suggested we stray off the trail a little way to explore something interesting, she cringed. Against her better judgment, she would follow me a couple hundred yards before insisting that we return to the trail.

Near the end of the trip, we met a man with his son and daughter (10 and 12 years old), who explained that they'd just come cross-country from an entirely different section of the forest. Using his map, they had cut their own trail and had seen some spectacular sights that he described.

My friend listened incredulously. How could someone do that? You could tell she thought he was crazy. Yet as he told his tale, something stirred inside of me. I yearned to explore the forest the way he had.

Some time later I had my chance to fulfill this desire in the Rockies. My parents live in a very secluded Colorado valley at 8000 feet, under East Spanish Peak. I had long ago looked up at that peak and decided I would climb it one day. The problem was that there was no trail leading to the top and I had no access to a map.

Others had tried it and ended up lost on the mountain for five days before a rescue party found them. People below had seen their night campfires at various points on the mountain during those five days. The valleys twirling off the peak are so confusing that it is extremely difficult to end up in the valley you are heading for, and the whole territory is so deserted that you are totally on your own.

Finally, the day came when, in spite of the warnings, I set out upon my cross-country climb through the lower valleys and up the peak. I told those who asked why, "I'm going up on the mountain in search of a burning bush." Somehow this climb was to be a spiritual-vision quest for me, and the image of Moses finding that burning bush seemed like a great archetype for my journey.

My parents' dirt road narrowed to a trail two miles up the way. The trail ended in a high meadow. I climbed over the fence that separated known from unknown and started "freelance" through the woods. I came upon a trail, a few rolling hills in, and decided to follow it. It carried me around the mountain but not up. Finally, I left it behind and headed straight uphill again.

Periodically, I would reach a high spot where I could view the peak and select which hills, valleys, and ridges I had to use to get where I wanted to go. Then I'd drop behind a hill or enter a wooded area where I'd have to blindly follow the route I had seen for those few moments until I reached another vantage point.

As I crossed the final ridge to the base of the last 3000-foot climb, a storm blew in. I was drenched. I found a spring from which to refill my water bottle and managed to cook a meal before the last climb. I was waiting for the rain to stop, but it didn't.

Finally, I set out to make the big climb, in spite of the rain. It was then that I found out why no one generally climbs East Spanish Peak. It's all rock and everything moves. It's an oversized gravel pit all the way up.

The pieces of rock ranged from 1 foot in diameter to 4- or 5-feet long, but each was precariously balanced, and I had to be careful where my steps were placed. The climb was almost straight up, and I was not sure I would ever make it. The air was thinner, my leg muscles threatened to give out at any moment, and the sun had fallen behind the mountain. I wasn't sure I knew how to get back, but right then all I cared about was reaching the top. There were trees interspersed among the rocks. I grabbed them to help pull myself up.

Surprising myself, I cleared the trees and ascended the final stretch to the top, just in time to see the sun set. The view from 13,000 feet was stupendous. I could see my parents' home far below, beyond dozens of hills and valleys. For a time I was lost in the glory of the height.

Then reality set in. I was wet and cold. A huge storm was moving in. I had intended to spend the night on top of the mountain, but I couldn't get a fire started, even with all my training. There was no place to roll out a sleeping bag, much less put up a tent. My down-filled bag wouldn't keep me warm since it was soaked. The wind was already at 50 miles an hour, and the temperature was dropping rapidly. In spite of exhaustion, I decided to head down the mountain with the little remaining light. Even if I didn't find home, it would be warmer at lower altitude.

I took one last look at my destination way below. The fog cleared for thirty seconds. I burned into memory the lay of the land and took a compass reading. Then the fog took control, and I could see no farther than 30 feet. I slid from tree to tree coming down the steep descent. Periodically, I'd suddenly come upon a 100-foot drop-off and have to go around it. I had the sense that God was with me each step. After all, I could have catapulted to death dozens of times.

By dark, I was off the mountainside and into the maze of hills, valleys, and ridges that lay between me and home. I groped my way through the woods remembering ups and downs, broken-down fence lines, and clearings as best I could. I constantly compared my path with the fluorescent glow of my compass.

At one point I came upon a path that seemed to lead where I wanted to go. It was a God-sent gift. When I decided I needed to depart from the path, I had only a short distance to go before I broke into a meadow and saw a narrow road I thought I recognized. I knelt on the road in the dark and felt, with my hands, a hump in the road that I hoped meant the road would lead to my parents' home. Two miles later, at 11:30 p.m., I trudged across the dam and into the house.

Some higher Force had led me home, and I had a trust in It that went beyond any I'd ever experienced before.

I had gone in search of a burning bush. I found a raging

storm. I endured the most strenuous physical test of my life. I gained a spiritual strength I cannot explain to others. In my desk today are written instructions on how to climb East Spanish Peak. They show the lay of the land, the paths you will cross that will lead you astray, and the ones that will lead you by the most direct route. They show the spring, woods, valleys, and fence lines plus give an idea of what to expect when you get there. I will go again one day. Maybe even take someone with me. After all, now I know the way.

EXPLORING THE SPIRITUAL WILDERNESS

A spiritual trek into the unknown is no less exciting or demanding than trailblazing on a physical mountain. The heights are even more glorious, and the knowledge gained is important to be recorded so others can go there. The same principles used to climb East Spanish Peak will be employed by the spiritual explorer as he or she pushes into the frontier. More important, the attitude of the trailblazer, whether physical or spiritual, is much the same. Without the explorer mindset, you can have all the tools of the trade and they will not take you to your destination.

There are two ways to hike through a wilderness. Many a backpacker is told to stick to the trail and follow the map. A few have curiosity and desire that lead them cross-country on their own adventure.

If you cringe at going cross-country, don't. Concentrate first on generating a desire for adventure which will triumphantly swallow your timidness and the belief that you are not up to the task. You will need to carry that thrill of adventure with you. Only that insatiable desire and the unreasonable knowing that a greater Force moves through you will enable you to persevere in the tough or the dry times. When the trip has been completed, in spite of any misery you might have gone through, you want to be able to say, "That was fun!"

THE FIRST PRINCIPLE

You are ready for spiritual trailblazing when, like that fool who climbed East Spanish Peak, you really want to approach a spiritual quality or experience one of the heights, in spite of the warnings. Thus you have the *first principle* of cross-country exploration: "Others have gotten lost or failed. You still want to try for it."

The real spiritual explorers are not intimidated by others' failed attempts. They glean what they can from their experiences and proceed. Warnings are merely helpful information to take on the journey; they are not a reason to turn back. Their own God-implanted desire is permission to succeed.

I admit to being frustrated by those who fearfully draw back from spiritual experience as well as those who blindly ignore warnings given to them. The first group miss the point of adventure entirely. The latter close their eyes in self-sabotage. Both approaches stem from fear.

Learn from others' failures. Listen to warnings. Don't accept fear. Don't let concerns dampen your confidence. Don't even accept them as valid until they are proven to be so. I suggest that you simply store them as preparedness, for they are the edge that may give you success.

When I climbed East Spanish Peak, I was careful in many ways that I would not have been, had I not known of the group which was lost for five days.

In the spiritual arena, I meditated upon the bottom chakra

in search of healing life force, despite warnings of the possibility of awakening overwhelming sexual desire that would be difficult to deal with. When I did encounter exactly that, the warnings served me well. Rather than trying to ignore this pestilence, I turned to face and conquer it before going on.

THE SECOND PRINCIPLE

The *second principle* of cross-country spiritual exploration is "Trails don't always lead where you want to go." They may just sidetrack you and go around the mountain. The trick here is to pick and choose.

There is no doubt that a defined spiritual path or one with instructions of a designated teacher is easier to walk than the tangled forest of untried experience. When you encounter such in the area that you have chosen to explore, the question you must ask is, Does this path lead to the mountaintop? If the answer appears to be yes, follow until it appears to be no.

Never pass up a well-worn path that appears to be going the right way. Just know when it is time to get off and freelance once again. Don't let your desire for the shortcut keep you a disciple longer than serves your own inner spiritual purpose. It's easy to become complacent, to get used to the shelter a path provides. Make sure the quest has really been altered if you decide to stay on that path and give up the mountaintop. However, if the path continues to head for the mountaintop, follow it all the way.

THE THIRD PRINCIPLE

I went in search of a burning bush. I found a raging storm. Thus a *third principle* might be "What you seek on the mountain may not be what you find on the mountain." Ponce de Leon went in search of the fountain of youth. He never found it. Yet what he did find changed the world.

The peak can look quite different from the valley floor than it does from the top. In fact, you may find this mountain has several summits, each with different views. The spiritual explorer is constantly striving for different perspectives. Seeming failure can be the path to success or the whip that turns us in a direction we shun but actually leads up the mountain.

With each experience, step outside yourself and try to look from a different direction at the path you are cutting. The light of this last step may cast a new shadow that points out a characteristic unseen before. The path you think you are walking will go through a number of transmutations. Roll with them.

Earlier I mentioned meditating on the bottom chakra in search of healing life energy. I had planned on missing the sexual desire that got released. However, it seemed to be part of the mountain. Dealing with it directly, I learned why Charles Fillmore had so often referred to the "sex lust" as being capable of robbing us of our life energy.

In a return "boxing match" with this energy, I succeeded in observing sexual energy fully without allowing it to carry me away. Shortly, intense sexual desire transformed into the most complete body rush of vitality and well-being I have ever experienced. It was no longer sexual, and it was evenly distributed throughout the whole body. The sexuality latent in the bottom chakra has never since been a problem for me, and I understand what is meant by "lifting" sexual desire.

This was a summit on the mountain I had not foreseen, an

adjoining piece of the energy I sought. It was like climbing the back side of the mountain called healing life force. It gave me a new vantage point from which to approach the original peak.

THE FOURTH PRINCIPLE

This brings us to a *fourth principle* of "Use vantage points." The freelancer cannot depend upon someone else's map. Yet periodically the explorer is given a glimpse of the energy or state of consciousness pursued. This is similar to those high vantage points where I would catch a glimpse of the peak, gauge the direction I had to go, and memorize the landscape I would have to traverse to reach the peak. Then, as I dropped behind a hill or moved into the woods, I would remember what I had seen, using it constantly until I reached another vantage point.

Proceeding through the spiritual practices you develop, you will have times when you feel as if you are getting somewhere. You can taste a little of what you are seeking. You may even have a single spiritual experience that then eludes you. As you go through the dry times when nothing seems to be happening, remember the vantage-point experience. Constantly strive to enter that consciousness through memory and use it as a base from which to do your present work. The dry times will urge you to abandon a seemingly fruitless effort. The vantage-point memory will keep you trudging forward one step at a time.

When you get your next glimpse of the spiritual realm to which you aspire, reassess your approach. You may have strayed off course slightly or you may see new approaches you haven't tried. Constantly contemplate all your breakthroughs. Add them together. Try to feel the flow of the path they have been leading you on. It all creates a connected picture, eventually.

Spiritual practice is the way you walk from one point to another. Your skill as an explorer is often measured by how creatively you can adapt these tools. If you've got to cross a river, you build a boat that you can paddle stroke by stroke to the other side. The spiritual explorer creates a practice that should serve the need and works with it.

Here the freelancer has an advantage over the path-bound disciple. The disciple considers everything he or she is taught as sacred, exactly the way the teacher presented it, and wouldn't dream of changing it. The explorer considers only the goal sacred and will borrow or bend a practice in any way that will prove helpful to the final goal.

THE FIFTH PRINCIPLE

The principle here is "Be creative!" There are some standby tools I'll go over in the next chapter but I suggest that you develop a knack for adapting them to your particular needs.

If you follow a teacher's instructions for a time, give the teacher the respect of following instructions as is until you experience what he or she is trying to show you. Having done that, you understand enough of what is truly important about what you've been doing to successfully adapt it to harmonize with the way you walk your path and to carry you toward the energy you desire. Remember anything that has worked. It can probably be adapted to other situations.

Creating a practice out of nothing is not that hard. Contemplate the spiritual energy state you seek. Imagine how you might use this energy, once attained, in your life. From that, devise ways to practice, trying to do the things you would do if you had already developed the quality. Open your mind to suggestions. Something will come to you.

Remember how important my compass was on the trip down the mountain in the dark. Constantly taking a compass reading is a cross-country principle all unto itself. We must explore so many cracks, crevices, and ravines along the way that dedicated explorers must constantly stop to ascertain whether or not the wonderfully interesting phenomena they are encountering are really leading them in the direction of their ultimate goals. The serious explorers continually choose to return to the goal, even when the distractions seem to be a lot more exciting.

The sliding rocks and sudden drop-offs of East Spanish Peak also have their lesson for spiritual explorers. The ascent to any serious spiritual height has its treacherous aspects. There are things to avoid and others that will just have to be endured. The pitfalls of ego and fantasy have already been addressed. Fear in its many disguises is a formidable adversary.

Pain and misery often go with the territory when stretching consciousness boundaries beyond the known and the comfortable. To the real trailblazer, it is all worth it. The gain is always worth any pain that may accompany it. In the end, pain and misery are only measurements of resistance to change. As such, they are manageable qualities.

Like the physical climber, the spiritual climber may find that everything he or she steps on moves. Learn to be comfortable in constant motion. We are creatures who love a stable foundation under our feet. When we are changing our sense of reality, nothing is stable.

Herein lies the real menace to the explorer. You may reach the height, gain the goal. If you do, you will most certainly rip the fabric of reality. The world will never be the same again. You can never return to life as you knew it. The explorer thrives on this, but he or she may go through a temporary state of devastation, nonetheless.

One spiritual climber unexpectedly found his heart shattered by a spiritual light that flooded his whole world and remained for four days. During this time a friend had to caretake him, help him through the mundane duties of life while he endured an ecstasy so intense that it created the most pain he'd experienced in his life.

All that love and beauty were more than he could take. He emerged from his experience shaken and changed forever. Reality as he had known it no longer existed. It is one thing to believe in expanded reality. It is entirely another to enter it through the shattered ruins of a world that once felt solid. Seven years later he still searches for the key to the experience that will never again allow him to be like others in this world.

This is a rather dramatic example of "reality tearing." It doesn't often take such an intense or lengthy form. If, however, you have the attitude of the trailblazer, this example will not scare you. It will intrigue you, even call to you.

THE SIXTH PRINCIPLE

The *sixth principle* could be stated: "Love the heights, but the real task is getting back down." No one goes up on a mountain to meditate, achieve illumination, and sit there in bliss for the rest of his or her life. The vision from the heights is always worth the agony of the climb. The explorer loves the heights. The breakthrough is the thrill he or she thirsted for.

It carries with it the responsibility of integrating this new energy into everyday life.

Some will return wanting nothing to do with everyday life. That only prolongs the adjustment period. The challenge now is to weave this energy into daily activities. Don't just leave it as a strange trip you once took.

It's also time to make your map, to record your journey. You went cross-country. You have a legacy to leave.

THE SEVENTH PRINCIPLE

The final ingredient of the trailblazer consciousness is the most important. This one can compensate for weaknesses in several other areas. Without it, successful cross-country travel is almost impossible.

I decided to climb East Spanish Peak because I believed to the depth of my being that God would guide me through the whole experience. Coming down the mountain in the dark, I knew I was terribly outclassed by the adversities I faced. Yet there was a strange calm that settled over my whole being. I did not make that trek alone. A Presence enveloped me. I still had to make competent decisions, field each little crisis, and painstakingly place one foot in front of the other for what seemed an eternity. But everything fell into place. Though I didn't know exactly how everything was going to unfold, I knew "God was there with me and God was in charge." *This is the seventh principle.*

This same attitude must accompany the spiritual explorer. Each time I've set out after the experience of a certain spiritual quality, I've known God would show me how to reach the goal. Though each spiritual journey has been a lot of work, things have always come together. God has always shown me my way through the maze.

The tools necessary to complete your consciousness climb will be provided along the way. Look for them. Keep aware. Start climbing. And trust the spirit that moves you along your path. It is because God knows the map that you don't need one.

Chapter 5

TOOLS OF THE TRADE

"I'm excited! I know exactly what spiritual frontier I want to go after. I'm sure it's what Spirit wants me to develop in my life. I'm not running off with stars in my eyes. I know it's going to be a lot of work. But I'm going to make a breakthrough if I really put my whole self into it!" Then there is a long pause. "So the only question left is, 'How do I get started?'"

Right here is where many would-be spiritual explorers stumble. They do all the visionary preparation, reach a height of expectation, and then they become bewildered trying to switch gears from "seeing" to "doing." Somehow, the distant glorious mountains appear so clear, they say, "Surely, I must already be there."

It is a real shock to move attention from envisioning the view from the summit to measuring how to traverse the hundred miles of grueling trail and deep ravines that lie between here and there. That first pitiful step onto the dusty trail is almost disheartening. Hoping for a grand shortcut that will catapult us along the way, we hesitate, searching the horizon, and say, "What shall I do?"

The first step is rarely grand, and yet it is the most important. Inertia must be overcome, and often, forward motion is created by applying one of those seemingly mundane basic tools such as prayer or meditation that we can always fall back on.

The same tools used to create that grotesque junior high school woodworking project are used by the skilled carpenter to create a valuable masterpiece. The skilled artisan may have added more complicated gadgets to a toolbox, but more than likely, still picks up the saw, hammer, tape measure, and screwdriver to kick off the process.

The intent of this chapter is to remind you of the basic tools of the spiritual explorer and discuss how to adapt them to the process at hand, until more creative practices unfold. Please remember, the power of a tool is not in how complicated or basic it is, but in the skill of the one who wields it. The same basic tools that started you down your spiritual path are still appropriate, even effective, in the hands of the adept traveling on the cutting edge.

Whenever we become bogged down and are not sure how to get going again, we should be able to reach into our bag of tricks and adapt one of those basic universal practices to meet the need. Trailblazing involves cutting our own path, but we are expected to take an axe or machete.

Our first step, the one that creates forward motion, will probably employ an utterly basic spiritual practice. Nothing is more basic than prayer, so let's begin there.

THE POWER OF PRAYER

Many years ago George (a man who would later become one of my spiritual mentors) found himself confined to a bed in a veterans hospital. He had somehow contracted a rare terminal illness for which there was no known cure. He was told that he would not emerge from this hospital. He would slowly get more and more debilitated and finally die. The prognosis was depressing, and for a while he became lost in hopelessness.

George finally decided to take a stand for healing, though he wasn't quite sure how to go about getting this healing. His options in terms of physical activities were quite limited. Ultimately, he decided he would tithe his time, committing six minutes out of each hour to praying for healing.

He prayed in all sorts of ways. Yet, no matter how he prayed, his commitment was to spend one-tenth of his day concentrating on healing in some manner. He would make up for the time he lost due to sleep by doubling up on his prayer work during waking hours.

George kept his prayer commitment, day in and day out, for weeks with no seeming results. After six or eight weeks, he started to feel a little stronger. Several months later, still tithing prayer time, he felt as healthy as he had ever felt. Surprisingly enough, X rays and lab results suggested a complete recovery. Since no one had ever made a comeback from this malady, George's doctors determined that his perfect health had to be an illusion which would vaporize soon. They kept him for two more months, when, still mystified, they finally released him.

George's training in healing was minimal, but he did have one simple tool in his arsenal: prayer. He used this tool with diligence and went right into the heart of that illusive spiritual energy we call healing. The experience deeply changed his life.

Along the way, George got creative. He varied his prayer activity through all kinds of approaches as ideas came to him. He started just by asking God to heal him. Later, he affirmed life and used imagery. All are simple, basic techniques. His intention was to find the source of life, a task worthy of the deepest mystic. Unrelenting prayer carried him all the way.

When you are ready to embark on your journey, while searching for the right in-depth practice to work with, start with prayer. Committed prayer time is the first tool in your box. It needs to be part of every search for spiritual break-through.

Ultimately, each spiritual practice you do could be labeled a form of prayer. When we break it down into "ways to pray," the simplest form is called "asking for help." It is often said that God is ready to come to your aid at any time if only you will ask.

In affirmative prayer, asking sounds like this: "Thank You, God, for my perfect healing." The classical approach is more like "Please God, heal my body." My experience has convinced me that either will work if the right feeling is put behind the words. After all, the real power behind a word is the energy one places in it.

THE POWER OF ASKING

The biblical suggestion "Ask, and ye shall receive" refers much more to a very special state of heart than to particular word groupings. Open your heart. Enter as sincere and humble a space as you can reach. Set ego completely aside. Image yourself having entered into the holy presence of the Almighty. Dropping all your walls, knowing you are in private audience with God, ask from the depths of your soul that God help you to attain your spiritual goal. Feel acceptance of God's will and gratefulness, no matter the outcome. Repeat this practice at regular intervals until guidance leads you to your next step.

The power of asking was illustrated clearly to me in the

experience of a friend, Wendy. She confided to me on the phone one day that she wanted to see Jesus' face. This seemed a strange primary spiritual goal to me, but she was adamant. "I want to see Jesus' face." In spite of my own questions about the project, I was supportive and asked her to let me know if she really got somewhere with this.

I was assailed by a number of philosophical concerns about her quest. For instance, I asked myself: "If Jesus is functioning within his resurrected celestial body, does this emphasis on a physical face have any valid meaning? The disciples on the road to Emmaus didn't recognize Jesus from his physical appearance. Couldn't he express through any form that served the need?" I understood being in Jesus' presence but had never experienced the presence as a face. Despite my own questioning, I hoped Wendy would get what she needed out of this search, and she did.

A couple of weeks later, Wendy called, excited: "I got the answer to my prayer! Jesus came to me in meditation last night."

"You mean you actually saw a face and knew it was Jesus?" I responded.

"I didn't actually see the whole face, but all of a sudden, two of the most loving, compassionate eyes came into focus. Waves of emotion rolled over me. Those eyes were captivating, and I knew it was Jesus. I could feel his presence all around me, and I knew I was his disciple. I'll never forget those eyes."

Intrigued, I asked, "What exactly did you do to bring this experience to you?"

Wendy replied, "Each evening as I started my meditation time, I would feel my deep desire to come face-to-face with Jesus and then I would ask to see Jesus' face. I would wait a few moments and then go on with meditation, knowing someday my request would be granted.

"Last night I did the same thing. Then, partway through my normal meditation time, Jesus' eyes unexpectedly came into focus. From there on, the experience was overwhelming and I felt a closeness to Jesus like I'd never felt before."

The intellect immediately wants to tear Wendy's experience apart. Did she really see Jesus' eyes, or did her imagination just create a picture? And of course, were those eyes blue or brown? None of that really matters. Wendy experienced her connection with Jesus Christ as her spiritual teacher in such a deep way: she knew what it meant to be Jesus' disciple on such a deep level that her life would never again be the same. She broke ground on the spiritual frontier. She accomplished it all by "asking" and continuing to ask.

Asking in prayer for the spiritual experience you seek is a standard practice that the explorer will use over and over to start his or her inward journey. It's basic, but effective.

THE POWER OF AFFIRMATION

The next tool to employ is affirmation. Many of us began our inner spiritual quest with such affirmations as these: *I live in the midst of abundance, God life is healing my body, divine order is established in all my life and affairs, God's wisdom guides me, I am drawing my perfect mate,* and *God is in charge of my life.* It is hard to imagine that such kindergarten practices will carry us to the cutting edge of spiritual discovery. Yet affirmation is one of the standbys for getting things rolling.

I used affirmation extensively during the early years of my spiritual awakening. Much later I realized I had shied away from the rote use of a simple statement over and over. It seemed that after years of study, I was more advanced than that. Affirmation was for beginners.

Farther down the path, I had to reassess this conclusion. After all, Eastern teachings were using *mantras* and *wazifas* to carry their disciples into the highest of spiritual experience. An affirmation is nothing more than a simple prayer statement used over and over. As such, it functions much as a mantra, except in English. Thus maybe there was a more skilled way to use this simple technique: something that went beyond an attempt to program the subconscious.

I remembered a retreat lecture given by Eric Butterworth. He had stated, "There are two types of affirmation: the programming statement and the power statement." He explained that with the programming statement one is attempting to put an idea into the subconscious mind. Repetition is supposed to aid this process. Repeating the affirmation hundreds of times eventually works, but each statement alone has little impact because it begins in the outer and is aimed at changing the level of mind that controls habitual thinking.

The alternate use of affirmation is the power statement. Here the energy travels in the opposite direction. One takes the statement of Truth into the heart and feels it to the depth of his or her being. When the experience reaches fullness, the words rise to the surface and are spoken aloud with the power of inner realization. An affirmation spoken once in this fashion carries more energy than a thousand programming statements.

Using this concept dredged up from memory, I began anew to work with affirmation. Soon I discovered that this primary technique goes far beyond kindergarten. The hammer and chisel remain the same, but they produce different results when used by the novice and the adept.

The higher use of affirmation first surfaced for me on a road trip many years ago. I had just driven two and a half hours to a large city airport to drop off two close friends who were journeying to their new home. It was a wonderful adventure, and I was happy for them. Yet I mourned their leaving. It would leave a gap in my life, at least for a little while.

I had driven my old pickup truck in order to transport all of their earthly belongings. It had no radio, and I contemplated the different ways I could entertain myself on the trip back. I could indulge in a long, drawn-out "I'm-so-sad-over-the-loss-of-my-friends" party. (Isn't it strange how we can actually enjoy an occasional side trip through misery?) I could let my mind run free, frolicking through TV sitcom plots, people encounters, imaginary happenings, and all sorts of meaningless tripe. Or a third possibility occurred to me: I could attempt to keep my mind centered on affirmations for two and a half hours, just to see if I could do it. I opted for the challenge of this third choice.

I selected the statement *My life is filled with love and joy!* and began the endurance test. My mind wandered shortly, and I dutifully brought it back to the task at hand. This happened several times before I considered that the problem lay in the fact that my affirmation, though spoken aloud enthusiastically, wasn't stirring up much energy to keep centered upon.

SPEAKING THE WORD

Realizing that I had, thus far, used only repetition (the programming affirmation), I decided to change my approach. I slowed down the words, striving to feel the meaning of each word as I spoke it. I would stop, momentarily, following the word *love* and attempt to feel the energy this word represented rising from the depths of my being. Likewise, I would stop after the word *joy*, reaching for the experience of that energy.

The first few times I was relatively unsuccessful, but after several tries, I was able to feel *love* for a fraction of a second after I spoke the word, then *joy* for a fraction of a second after I spoke that word. Now the practice gained in excitement. With each cycle, I could feel the energies grow stronger and last for a longer time. Eventually, the experience began with the actual speaking of the word as well as following it. The result was electrifying.

I decided to strengthen the statement: *I am filled with Love and Joy.* The affirmation was evolving as I absorbed more of the divine energies and realized my declaration could ascend to a higher form.

After an hour of affirming in this expanded way, without my attention wavering once, I was saturated with love and joy. I could have gone another hour, but I became enthusiastic about adding another energy to my repertoire. I headed for an affirmation of confidence. Then an affirmation of my relationship as a child of God.

By the end of the journey, I had succeeded in affirming for two and a half hours straight. The experience of expanded affirmation was so compelling that success had not required great effort. This was a new way to use this basic tool that I intended never to forget. I emerged from my pickup floating on air and maintained this spiritual high for days.

Since that time, I have continually depended upon this form of affirmation to kick off spiritual exploration as well as to fall back on it when I get bogged down.

The key to powerful affirmation is to feel the most important words with special emphasis. Reach inward for the energy experience that these selected words are meant to convey. Each word is spoken as if you have called someone's name and are listening attentively within yourself for the sound of approaching footsteps. Even if you have no idea what that spiritual energy will actually feel like, your vigilance will eventually be rewarded by the sense of "approaching footsteps" and, finally, the actual presence of the spiritual experience you are calling.

Choose a short, simple, direct statement about your objective. Select your primary word or words carefully. Often several words will describe the spiritual experience you seek. List them all. Try out the list to determine which is the strongest or piques the most feeling for you. Sometimes the classic word in the list feels overused or worn out. If this is the case, select a fresh one that has more spark.

The selected focus word should be surrounded by a sentence that clearly states the goal in full completion. Include an *I am, me,* or *my life, my mind, my heart, my body,* and so on, to pull it out of the abstract into personal experience. Use *God, Divine, Spirit, the Almighty, the Christ,* and so on, in your statement to connect your goal to its true source. You can also do this by using a God-word to modify the energy you seek, such as *Divine Love, God's love,* or *the love of the Almighty.* A shortened version is to speak only the word for the spiritual energy you seek, such as *Love, Joy, Life,* and *Abundance,* realizing each time that this is truly another name for God.

Put the affirmation together in a succinct statement that ties you to God by way of the spiritual experience to which you aspire. Divide the affirmation into words or phrases that can be accompanied by separate inner experiences of what the words mean.

As you speak each phrase, reach inward to try to experience the energy you have named or the image of action created by the words. Pause to feel an experience accompanying the words. Then move to the next phrase and reach for the feeling experience that these new words describe. When you finish, start the cycle of words and feelings again. Strive for a more expanded inner experience each time you affirm.

Examples of how this process might be used could be as follows:

God's love fills my heart. God's love—feel the all encompassing warmth of God's love as you speak these words. *Fills my heart*—allow that energy to funnel into your heart, concentrate, and then overflow into the world around you.

I am a fountain of Divine Life. I am—move to the very center of your being. *A fountain*—feel a flow opening and bubbling forth within you. *Of Divine Life*—feel that bubbling essence as pure life of God flowing throughout your whole being.

I live in the kingdom. I live—center your energies and draw your awareness of your life to this center. *In the kingdom*—let the sense of wealth in all things tangible and intangible burst into awareness within you and all around you. In this instance, the word *kingdom* is used as the name for God's state of absolute abundance in all things.

Divine Will takes command of my will. Divine Will—sense the part of God that directs all creation toward the highest good of the whole. *Takes command*—feel it moving with absolute authority. *Of my will*—surrender before this movement of absolute authority. Feel your desire diminishing and

a higher, nobler presence taking hold of your being to use it for
God's purposes.

I am at peace. I am—move to the center of your being. *At
peace*—peace here is another name for God's presence. Feel
this divine energy state released in the midst of you, quieting
all discord, and nurturing you on the deepest levels.

As you see, there are an infinite number of applications of
this process. Make each repetition of the words an attempt to
feel the energies involved and their movements through you.
The more times you repeat the process, the greater depth of
meaning each word or phrase will carry for you. There is far
too much going on to get bored.

THE POWER OF IMAGERY

The next most useful tool for awakening spiritual experience is imagery. Like its brother, affirmation, it can be
approached from different depths.

One begins by steadily holding in mind a visual image that
expresses the chosen area of spiritual realization. This becomes
a prayer statement in picture form. Once again, power is
instilled in the practice by adding the feeling aspect.

If your objective were to touch divine healing life, you
would begin with affirmation and reach inward to feel the
energies of the words. Then you would augment this with an
image of that healing life filling your being. You might visualize divine life as a white light descending from the heights of
Christ consciousness through the top of your head and flowing into every section of your body. You might further see this
light of life flowing through your mind, infusing all of your
thoughts.

If you have a hard time making these pictures appear in

your mind's eye, realize that imagery doesn't have to be strictly visual. In fact, it needs to become much more than a picture to be effective. We have all manner of ways to perceive—seeing, hearing, smelling, feeling, tasting, sensing in that sixth-sense way, and ultimately, knowing that a thing is happening. Effective imagery uses all of these forms of perception to transport you into the experience. If a visual picture eludes you, concentrate on a level of perception that comes naturally to you.

Many years ago I learned the power of concentration through visualization when someone suggested I try the simple spiritual practice of seeing myself glowing in light. Actually, I thought the practice was oversimplified at first but changed my mind after using it. The entire instructions were to see yourself glowing in light and continue to do so for twenty minutes.

I decided to devote my nightly meditation to this. I began by visualizing my body glowing in light and the radiance reaching out a foot or two in all directions. The image was partly "visual," partly "feeling" or "sensing" light around me, and a great deal of "knowing" that I was glowing in light.

At first it was quite a task to keep my attention on this inner image. I continually had to return my mind to the perception of body radiance. Success seemed to depend upon discipline and will.

After ten or fifteen minutes of sustained visualization, there was a shift in the character of the meditation. Suddenly, I was no longer trying to see myself glowing in light. I was no longer using will to keep an image in mind. I was experiencing the radiance of my being, naturally and effortlessly. I found myself joyously in the midst of realization of the divine Light, of my spiritual Self. What began as imagery opened the door to the real experience.

How do I know it wasn't a momentary fantasy? I had a quiet, deep knowing that makes the experience more real than the physical world. Yet beyond this, the spiritual hangover lasted the whole next day. Everything flowed. I got ready in the morning with a half hour to spare. I accomplished all of my tasks that day in half the normal time. Everywhere I went, order prevailed and events seemed to coordinate almost miraculously.

The objective of imagery is not to create a spiritual fantasy world. It is to use the image held in mind as a point of concentration until we are able to embrace the real experience of a higher energy. This real experience will likely not be just as you visualized it. At the very least, the richness and character of the energy will be a pleasant surprise as it carries you far above your feeble attempt to capture it in an image. Realization changes your life. Anything short of that is fiction.

Many people are so eager for immediate success that they settle for fantasies of spiritual realization. Real results may come quickly, or they may demand years of striving. Question seeming success that doesn't show results in your life. Continue with your practices until you break through fantasy to the real spiritual experience that lies beyond.

Up to now, we have described imagery as static concentration. In this usage, it is the equivalent of an affirmation in picture form. When this tool is extended into the state of meditation, called *contemplation*, it becomes fluid. It can carry the experience gained from affirmation to a deeper, more intense level.

In contemplation, the mind (having been disciplined through concentration) is given freedom to think about the spiritual objective and see what it can discover. If love were the focus, the creative side of mind would be allowed to contemplate the ways love could express in one's life, the results a flow of love might create, what it would feel like to have this energy flowing through one on a constant basis, and so on.

Fluid imagery becomes the natural extension of mental contemplation as all manner of pictures and scenarios arise out of the creative part of mind. Pictures evolve into other pictures. Scenarios become imaginary journeys, leading to places we haven't consciously planned to visit. Experiences evolve, changing along with the visual progression. Eventually, something triggers a breakthrough and the inner play dissolves under the onslaught of higher energies.

In practice, we would begin with an affirmation, concentrating on the flow of energy that the words describe. When we feel something, we would allow inner creativity to supply images or a journey that expresses the feeling we've been able to touch. Or we contemplate the possibilities surrounding the energy we've been striving for and create an imaginary scenario that helps us explore our mental perceptions in regard to this spiritual objective.

For example, a number of years ago I decided I wanted to isolate the spiritual energy that created abundance and integrate it firmly into my consciousness. The first step was to choose the main word and create an affirmation. I concluded that *abundance* was an overused and stale word for me. I finally settled on *plenty* because it felt fresh and carried a charge for me. *My life is filled with plenty* became my affirmation.

Each day I would crawl up on the roof of my house (where I was doing my meditation at that time) and begin by repeating this statement: *My life is filled with plenty*. I would stop to feel the energy of the word *plenty* with each declaration. Then I would move into a contemplation stage and consider what a life filled with plenty would mean and how it would feel. From the contemplated feeling of plenty, I evolved a vision which seemed to embody that feeling.

I would see myself walking down a road, the path of my life. This road stretched into the infinite future, winding around hills and going all manner of places I couldn't see from where I walked. Yet I knew that around every bend, God had a wonderful surprise for me.

I could feel the gifts coming to me. As I walked down this path, I claimed each gift, though it didn't necessarily take a certain form. I would keep sensing all the new surprises coming to me. I walked through this visualization for extended periods of time each day for six weeks.

One day, in the midst of this visualization journey, an overwhelming energy surged out of my heart and overwhelmed me with emotion. I realized: This is it! This is the energy of abundance.

The energy swept over me, shattered the visualization, and carried me upward of its own accord.

In the midst of my ecstasy, I thought, How will I describe this energy? I realized it was hauntingly familiar. It was almost like something I already knew. The word finally came into focus. It was *gratefulness*—overwhelming gratefulness. Weave that energy into your consciousness and you will know abundance.

It was the fluid image that had taken me to the doorway of realization and pushed me through. This tool has thousands of adaptations. As you reach for any of the heights, create an image that expresses where you want to go and let it evolve.

Like affirmation, the imaginary journey is repeated over and over. Each time, it etches a deeper experience. The same fluid image can be used repeatedly, or the journey can be unique and new each time. If the vision changes, the process that creates the journey remains constant. In this way, each imaginary experience still revolves around the same original objective. Eventually, enough energy gathers to allow you to break beyond imagery into the real spiritual experience.

I will briefly address one, last basic tool. It is abstract and difficult to capture in words. In subtle ways though, it carries tremendous power. I call it "the intent of your being."

THE POWER OF INTENTION

Intention is a powerful mind energy. It seems to override verbal meanings and even visual images as long as the underlying intent is clear and strongly held.

A Native-American medicine man once interviewed a potential patient. His most important question was "Why do you want to be healed?" The healer went on to explain that "I just want to feel better" would not be a good enough answer. The injured man explained what he wanted to do with his life, how he would serve if he were able to move freely again. The medicine man finally decided there was enough "purpose" in the man's desire to be healed to warrant the efforts of his healing ceremony.

By first asking the aspirant to state clear intention, the Native-American healer set a precedent that all spiritual explorers should follow. When embarking upon a journey of spiritual awakening, we must ask ourselves two questions: "What purpose will this awakening serve?" and "How intent am I upon this goal?"

The first question reminds us of our commitment to serving the whole. If our purpose lies only in personal gratification, intent is attached to a weak objective and the odds favor failure. We need to be very clear about why we seek success and what we would do with it.

The second question deals with our level of commitment to the path when faced with increasing difficulties. Here again, we must know that we have an unswerving will to awaken this spiritual experience in our lives. We must connect the entire purpose of our existence to the spiritual awakening we seek. We must know that we will endure through seeming failure for as long as it takes to reach success.

To place the intent of your being upon a goal, first place your will on the objective. If healing life were your objective, you would declare to yourself, "My intention is to awaken healing life." You would feel the energy of will pouring out of your forehead and attach it to "awakened healing life," a goal that visually lies before you. That pathway of intention becomes like an unbreakable cord which now attaches you to the objective.

If the objective, healing life, is firmly attached to higher purpose, your cord of intent is attached to a mountain that cannot be moved. If your commitment is to stick with your task until achieved, no matter how long it takes, the cord cannot be broken. It acts like a tractor beam that slowly, yet unyieldingly, draws you toward the awakening experience.

Intention is more than will. Will can tire. Intention perseveres, even through extended periods of seeming failure. Feel the attachment of will to start the process. Then align desire from every level of your being along the cord of intent. Fix the intent of your whole being upon the spiritual goal and know that once you have done this, you will be moving toward the objective whether you are consciously thinking of it or not.

It is not your will trying to force an outcome. It is not your conscious thought or your subconscious patterns creating the result. It is not your desire alone drawing you forward. It is all of the above and much more. Your entire being has the quiet, easy, steadfast knowing of where you are going. Your purpose in living is fulfilled by achieving the goal. Thus all the spiritual forces in the world are drawing you toward awakening. God is leading you upon a path uniquely designed for this particular spiritual discovery.

Your individual efforts come from a different level entirely. The intent of your being, once attached to the objective, functions effortlessly, using everything in your life to lead you to the goal. You will remember your intention on a regular basis to reinforce your efforts. Yet once established, the intent of your being functions very much on its own, with or without your conscious concentration.

Events that seem to veer away from success mysteriously work together to draw you closer to awakening. Long periods of "hitting a blank wall" finally abate, leaving you on higher ground. It all becomes part of one flow, winding its way toward the goal and tied together by your overall intent.

Once you have reached out and embraced your spiritual aspiration with the intent of your being, success is ensured. All that is left is negotiation of time and effort. You gently know that everything you encounter in life will make a contribution toward your awakening. Often this will happen in ways you cannot fathom.

Any spiritual journey worth taking deserves your full cooperation by attaching to it the intent of your being. Total commitment is a tool to be used in all cutting-edge exploration.

Chapter 6

CREATING PRACTICES

Taking a covered wagon West in the American pioneer days was quite a feat. Common people became adventurers. They would follow the roads over bridges and through all manner of landscapes. They would occasionally come upon a river where they had to pay the ferryman to transport them to the other side.

Then, finally, the roads would end. The prairies stretched out in front of them. Weeks from nowhere, they would come upon a river with no bridge or ferry. They would search up- and downstream for a shallow crossing. When there was no crossing to be found, they had to get creative.

In many cases, they would design a raft. They would fell the trees and anchor them together. Then they would pole across to the other side or secure a rope and pull across. Some lashed logs directly to the sides of the wagon, enabling it to float half-submerged. It was done a number of different ways, but each pioneer designed his or her own medium for getting to the other side.

Spiritual pioneering works much the same way. When the road ends and you come to a formidable river to cross, you first look for a bridge or a ferry—some spiritual practice that is designed to move you across the river to the higher experience. When none is to be found, you build your own raft. You create a practice with which you can work in order to get results.

There are all kinds of ways to design a practice. You may remodel something that worked in another area. You may think up an approach you've never tried before. The key to success is having the courage to be creative.

Every spiritual journey starts with basics. Often though, we require very specific application of the energies we stir up with these basics in order to harness them and weave them into our consciousness. Each quest presents its own set of parameters.

Success requires us to figure out how to use the insight our basic tools expose. This usage may be unique to this particular spiritual experience. Practice in this usage brings the experience out of the rare and unusual into a normal and automatic expression of life.

Just as the pioneer abandons the raft when the wagon rests solidly on the far shore, we will drop practices when we have worked the higher light into our everyday consciousness. The spiritual experience then continues with us automatically. It is part of who we are.

The practices are not sacred—only the higher energy they are designed to touch. Thus practices can be altered, added together, or simply created out of our imagination. They are a means to an end. Anything that works qualifies.

As an initiate in a certain mystical order, I learned a whole array of spiritual practices. I worked with them as taught until I understood what they accomplished. However, some employed foreign languages and others antiquated traditions that seemed unnecessary.

As a spiritual teacher in my own right, I learned to share with others what I had learned by salvaging the most important aspects of the practices and substituting common language or shortened, modern approaches. Soon I discovered that the adapted practice was quite effective at accomplishing the purpose for which I had created it.

My teachers within the order would have been horrified, but the updated practices worked beautifully for people who wouldn't have touched the traditional version.

As I headed out solo into the spiritual frontier, my hobby of altering practices to serve the need at hand became a real asset. When I hit a wall on a spiritual search, I'd remodel an old practice, apply it directly to the task at hand, and chip away at the wall.

Finally, I became confident enough to create my own practices, tailored to the specific consciousness jump I was attempting. Sometimes they worked. Other times they didn't. But slowly I got the hang of it. I came to realize that it's really quite easy to create your own medium for making the jump.

It took me years to learn to trust myself in this area, but you can skip all that. I'll share with you some of the basic patterns you can fall back on when you are stumped. Beyond that, the instructions read, "Be creative and trust yourself." The key ingredient to designing your own practice is accepting that you can. You must have the courage to tap creativity and know your product will not be inferior.

REMODELING

The first and most often-used approach to creating your perfect spiritual practice is called "Remodeling." Why reinvent the wheel when you can simply bolt it to a new cart?

Everyone interested in spiritual exploration has reached this point by way of different spiritual practices that have gotten results. There have been meditation techniques, ways to pray, imagery techniques, things to do, and all manner of other special techniques that captured our imagination along the way. They are fun. They have a specific format. There is mystique in the intricate instructions that accompany them.

Look over your gathering of techniques: journaling, writing a letter to God, treasure mapping, listing goals on index cards and going over them each night, repeating affirmations a certain way, taking a specific imaginary journey in meditation, concentrating on the seven chakras in a certain way prior to meditation, taking an affirmation while you breathe in and another while you breathe out, centering on a thought in meditation and then letting go, seeing energy radiating out of your hands, and so on. You may want to write down everything you've done over the years. This is your erector set. You can tear them apart, change them, and put them together in whatever way serves your present purposes.

Treasure mapping is a basic-level prosperity technique in which the spiritual student makes a poster on which he or she places pictures of all the goals to be achieved. The poster is hung on the wall where it can be seen each day. This technique generally emphasizes concrete, easy-to-picture objectives. One might throw in a few spiritual words to cover the intangible desires.

A friend of mine adapted this basic technique to her journey into the frontiers. She created a scrapbook that was combination spiritual journal, treasure map, and list of affirmations. She would create pictures that represented abstract qualities she aspired to uncover. Each page had an affirmation that she used along with the picture to bring the spiritual energy into focus. Pages were then devoted to carefully thought-out affirmations that represented her prayer requests for herself and others. She wrote them around angel pictures by her favorite spiritual artists.

Each evening she would enter a reverie by quietly leafing through the pages of the pictorial and verbal representation of her spiritual journey. There's nothing earth-shattering or unusual in any of this, but it was a remodeled combination of a lot of simple things she had done in the past. It worked for my friend, and her spiritual progress is enviable.

When you are trying to get from hither to yon and need a vehicle for creating a breakthrough, examine techniques you've used for other spiritual demonstrations. If it worked once, it can probably be redesigned to serve another purpose. Plug in different words or new pictures. Change the activity, but keep the same general purpose of the practice. Take things you like from several practices and put them together. Cut and paste to your heart's content, but create an activity that enables you to focus on the spiritual experience you are pursuing.

CREATING AN ORIGINAL PRACTICE

Adapting a past practice can be a wonderful approach, but we are not restricted to altering known territory. A second approach is to create something entirely original. You might engineer a meditation pattern that should lead to a certain higher energy. Create your own rituals that will express the sought-after experience. Design a pattern to follow with open-ended areas where each meditation time can become unique. Along the way, you will hone and redefine your pattern in order to emphasize what works.

However, the easiest way to create an original spiritual practice is to harness a normal life activity to your specified spiritual purpose. Ask yourself: "What gut-level life experience will be affected by the development of this divine energy? What can I do to prove to myself that this energy is flowing through my outer life?"

As an example, a number of years ago I set out to conquer a certain fear. For much of my life, I had traveled under the fear of rejection by the opposite sex. The more attracted I was to a woman, the more intense the fear became.

This fear had affected my behavior patterns for years and was now standing in the way of spiritual progress.

In meditation, I realized I could no longer put off confrontation with this personality flaw. I made the commitment to face my fear until it was gone, no matter whether it took two months or ten years.

The next question was "How?" In meditation, I adapted a technique of following the feeling back through memories to try to find its source. I affirmed and imaged this fear removed. I remembered times in which I had reacted out of this fear and tried to release the hold its energy had on me.

Thinking like a coach, I decided to create training sessions in which I would face the fear and grapple with it. I set up my training in normal life situations.

The first training exercise came from the realization that I naturally encountered this fear (even if it didn't show) quite regularly throughout a week. I determined to recognize the negative energy every time it came up and to attempt to release it.

Deciding this first practice wasn't intense enough, I devised a second level of training. On a regular basis, I set myself up to ask out women who I knew would not accept the invitation. Often I selected someone who would not know me well enough to logically accept. I always chose a woman to whom I was attracted in order to lift my fear level. Most of these individuals played their role perfectly.

I often looked like a fool, but each time I went through my exercise, I gained a little more control over my fear level. I treated each experience as an experiment in which I was striving for a comfort level while facing fear of rejection directly. Thus success was not actually getting a date. Success was feeling comfortable within myself, no matter what was said during the exchange.

It took a year for the knot in my stomach to release. I remember the day when the energy of all of those past experiences left me. My training sessions in everyday life played a strong role in that final success. This all may seem strange to some, but for me it was a spiritual practice created to serve a very specific purpose. And it worked.

Another example of creating a practice from outer life comes from my work on developing intuition. One day while searching for a new training tool in the area of intuition, my most recent hobby caught my attention. I had become interested in watching the stock market and decided to turn this into a spiritual experiment. For a spiritual practice, I started consulting my intuition each day about whether or not a certain stock or mutual fund would go up or down. It was the perfect vehicle for measuring intuitive knowing. I could read the results in the newspaper the next day.

I could have just as easily devised a practice of guessing who was on the phone each time that it rang, but this worked for me. It was something that I enjoyed.

Shortly I decided to intensify the practice by actually investing my little bit of savings according to the guidance I received. Putting my money where my mouth was took the experiment out of the nonthreatening abstract and added the stress of real life.

Success was tied to learning about intuition, not to making money. During the year I used this practice, I carried my awareness of divine intuition to new depths. I learned to touch the quiet knowing of real guidance and to identify the energies of fear, personal desire, and logic that parade as guidance.

I made 30 percent on my investment in spite of some strong losses while I was learning to identify the false voices within. Yet the real gain of that year was my increased ability to receive and trust guidance. This practice, created out of mundane material life, accomplished its spiritual mission admirably.

Whatever your spiritual aspiration, no matter how abstract, there is probably some activity in your outer life that can be used to create a practice which will carry you there. Change the objective of the activity to relate to your spiritual goal. Then devise a program that will turn the whole thing into a training session for developing the higher energy.

Jesus was born in a stable. Likewise, the outer material life can be used as a vehicle for birth of the higher Christ energies.

Inner practices are created around patterns. If you understand the pattern, it can be applied to almost any spiritual goal. In a moment of inspiration, you may conceive of a meditation pattern that will carry you to a breakthrough. When this inspiration grabs you, put it to work. Any new pattern is a valuable commodity.

On the other hand, I have worked with several tried-and-true meditation patterns that are versatile enough to be applied to almost anything. I fall back on them constantly and believe you'll find them useful.

One of them centers around reducing your goal to one word. I call this practice "Developing a Christ Quality," and it begins with an exercise in focusing.

DEVELOPING A CHRIST QUALITY

Spiritual goals are often abstract. We know the general area that calls to us but are vague about what this particular experience will actually be like. Even when we know what we are seeking, we are often wordy in our attempt to define it.

As your first step in quiet meditation, attempt to reduce your objective to one word. Make it as specific a word as you can find. Sunlight brought to pinpoint focus with a magnifying lens generates a lot of heat. Spiritual aspiration brought to pinpoint focus as one word carries a lot of power. Contemplate what one word best embodies the spiritual experience you seek. Try each one. With your feeling nature, weigh which word is where you want to go. In the end, a word will feel right. Choose it, and focus on it.

The focusing process is aided by taking a certain perspective. I have come to the conclusion that everything we desire in life ultimately can be broken down into different spiritual energies, or Christ qualities.

For example, we think we want someone to love us. In actuality, we yearn for that feeling of love we get inside when we believe someone loves us. We think we want healing. In reality, we want to feel ourselves immersed in that divine energy of eternal, unstoppable life from which healing flows. We are convinced we want a new car, a nice house, and a flush bank account. In the end, we want the ecstasy, the security, and the comfort that we think wealth will provide. We want the energy state of abundance.

Every objective in life can be broken down into the inner energy state that underlies it. In your focusing process, use this realization to come up with your word.

You are after an energy. Life, love, wealth, joy, freedom, beauty, release, oneness, silence, confidence, purpose, and so on—all can be viewed as spiritual energies out of which very specific desires and activities flow. The energy is what you feel at the deepest level while you successfully enter the activity or state of circumstances you contemplate. Learn to generate the energy and everything else flows.

Once you have completed the focusing step by naming the energy you pursue, your second step is to begin concentrating upon this Christ quality. Repeat the word over and over, attempting to feel the energy it represents. Eventually, you want to be able to isolate this particular inner state and generate the feeling of it simply by calling the word.

You take the pattern a third step by carrying the word into contemplation. Image the activities that this energy will flow through. Contemplate how it could be channeled into outer life.

The fourth step comes when you are able to immerse yourself in the energy and simply experience it in a timeless, wordless inner state.

Once you can generate the inner feeling even a little, it's time to harness it. The fifth step is to awaken the spiritual energy and apply it to life by doing things while in this state. Eventually, you will become conversant enough in this Christ quality to weave it (to some degree) into your everyday consciousness.

These five steps have worked for me over and over. They are versatile enough to be applied to almost any spiritual quest.

JUMP STARTING

The third practice I fall back on could be called "Jump Starting." One can start an automobile that has a dead battery by "jumping" from the battery of a car which is already running. Sometimes you can get the impetus you need to break through a barrier to spiritual progress by "jump starting" from the memory of a strong, life-changing experience you've already had.

This process is quite simple. In meditation, remember your highest, most dramatic spiritual experience. Go over each detail with particular attention to the feelings, the realizations, and the elevated perceptions that you experienced. Relive the awe, the knowing, the overwhelming emotions, and the unfathomable part of your experience. In this way, you should be able shortly to transport yourself (at least partially) to that high state of consciousness in which the original event took place.

When memory brings back the elevated energy state, immediately switch your focus to the quest before you now. Continue with whatever practices you are employing or listen for insight into a new approach. Repeat the jump start whenever you lose momentum.

BREATH, LIGHT, OR SOUND

Another standby for creating practices is to employ "Breath, Light, or Sound." All three seem to intensify the power of any concentration. You still have to come up with some means of using these ingredients. However, sometimes when you know what you are going to put into it, any suitable container will do. Look over whatever tool you are already using (like affirmation, imagery, prayer, or a particular meditation approach) and determine how you could expand them to include work with breath, light, or sound.

Breath might be included by silently taking one affirmation as you breathe in and another as you breathe out. Or you could attempt to breathe in the divine quality you are concentrating on and then radiate it into the world as you breathe out. You could use your breath as an instrument, striving to tune your rate and type of breath to the spiritual experience for which you are reaching.

A slow, deep breath might be used to carry you to depths where outer life is far behind and spiritual experience close at hand. Alternately, a dynamic "holotropic" breath (rapid breathing combined with music or sound) could be employed to charge your system with energy for reaching new heights. If you are aware of the different energies produced by different styles of breathing, you may wish to attune the appropriate type of breath to your present objectives. In any case, the attempt to coordinate the spiritual rheostat of breath to your practices generally encourages results.

Light is even easier to incorporate. After all, everything connected with God can be imaged as light. A healing can be experienced as light descending through the body, a glow awakening in every cell. Guidance can seem like light infusing your mind. Prayer can be described as a pathway of light.

You could use light to behold an awakened heart, a divine energy entering your being, or a glowing state of living in the kingdom. You can rise into the higher realms of Light to experience oneness with God, see your higher Christ Self as a

Being of Light, or use the consciousness of Light as a background in order to ascend to realization of a Christ quality. You can radiate a certain quality to others on a beam of light. Any concentration on light should lift your awareness to higher levels where your spiritual aspirations seem more accessible.

Sound makes the heaviest outer impression on your being. Speak your focus word or your affirmation aloud and listen to the way it physically moves the energies of the room. Feel the texture the sounds produce. Try to feel the spiritual energy you desire in your consciousness and practice pouring that energy into your voice. Sing your affirmations and allow the tune to change as your understanding of them deepens.

Music can be used to draw you toward the state you desire or to tear away at the barriers you feel inside. A single ringing note can pierce the being, ripping away the walls of normal consciousness and carrying you into an altered state where you have less resistance to a higher experience. Sound is like a hammer. We revert to it when faced with the truly stubborn obstacles.

ENERGY WORK

A fifth member of our spiritual-practice erector set is "Energy Work." Here we exercise the atrophied muscles of our spiritual body. This type of practice can be more like creating a game with a purpose. If you are studying healing, you may want to play at radiating the realization of healing to everyone you pass. If opening your heart, reach out and see if you can surround with love someone across the room or at a great distance. You may try to bring peace to a roomful of people by holding yourself firmly in a peaceful consciousness while you reside in that room.

I am sure you get the idea. Create a game out of moving a spiritual energy into the world around you. If you get no results at first, don't worry. The mere act of playing the game can often awaken a higher experience.

A more serious side to this area of spiritual work is to coordinate actual concentration on the major energy centers and subcenters of your spiritual body (see Fillmore's *The Twelve Powers*) with the spiritual experience you seek. Certain spiritual energies are given body locations to aid focus when trying to awaken them. If you concentrate on one or several of these centers in your practice, you can expect to see increased results.

You may wish to see each center glowing in light to build your energy level prior to setting course for your current destination.

If you can connect your present goal to a particular center, concentrate on it as a part of the awakening. For example, if you are developing divine love, concentrate on the heart. If you want to "see clearly," affirm it as you focus yourself in your third eye center. Rise through your crown center at the top of your head in order to rise above your human limitations and merge with God. If you have done work with your spiritual energy centers, you can incorporate their energies into your practices.

If spiritual body and energy centers are an undeveloped area, you might consider making a journey into this territory and doing some exploring. Once they are exercised a little, these energy centers are very useful on many inward expeditions.

ROLE-PLAYING

My final suggestion for creating spiritual practices is a process I'll call "Role-Playing." Mundane as it sounds, this area includes some of the most sacred practices I have used. These techniques are based on the principle of imitating a height until you can actually scale it.

To begin, imagine that you have already achieved your aspiration. Then try the role. Examine what it feels like to function within this higher state of illumination. What kind of activities will this higher state stimulate? When an activity occurs to you, do it just as you would if you were truly in that state. You can, at least, live it out in your mind. It helps if you can add a physical aspect to your exercise such as walking down the street or looking into people's eyes.

If your aspiration were to reduce the barriers between yourself and others, merging with them in an instant and knowing what each was thinking, you would role-play this state. In your mind, quietly go through life looking into each face and knowing each person's hopes and sorrows. Experience the responsibility this awareness places on you and the integrity it requires of you. Cope with decisions of when and how to act on the knowledge you have with the restraint that wisdom would require. Experience the total acceptance necessary of someone who views people's selfish, cruel, or violent thinking without passing heavy judgment upon them.

A further step in the role-playing is to actually take a walk among people while acting out this scenario in your mind. Thus real people play parts in your fictitious process (though they don't know it). This makes the feelings seem more real for you. You must walk and move as someone who lives in this higher consciousness. During the role-playing exercise you will often gain significant insight or feel you have actually touched the energy you have been imitating.

Many years ago I decided to try to view the world as God

sees it. Everything was my beloved creation; every person was my dearest child. It was a long stretch, but I figured it would be worth the effort. Shortly I determined to expand the exercise by going outside and walking down the street. Everything I looked at, I cherished and loved as mine. Everyone I passed was my deeply loved child. I attempted to feel what it must be like to be loving Father to all life.

It took all the concentration I could muster and, of course, I fell short. Even as imperfect as it was, I could keep the role-playing up for only a couple of blocks. Yet this exercise had a dramatic effect upon my perceptions. I experienced an energy state I cannot really explain, but it has haunted me ever since. Those short moments provided one of those memories I can use in the jump-start process described earlier.

THE WALKS OF THE MASTERS

There is a classic mystic practice used throughout the ages that specifically employs the role-playing process. It is called "The Walks of the Masters."

The way you walk conveys a lot about the state of consciousness you are expressing. When you are feeling confident and peaceful with the knowledge that nothing can shake you, you will walk with a certain gait and flow to your movement. When you are feeling rushed, insecure, and overwhelmed by life, your walk will take on a different gait and flow. The body moves according to the energies that are expressed through it.

For "The Walks," disciples imagine they are one of the great masters. Once they begin to feel what it is like to be this illumined being, they begin to walk (possibly in a circle). As they move, they attempt to feel the particular attributes or consciousness of the master they contemplate, directing the flow of the body. Thus there is continual feedback between body sensation and inner imitation of consciousness. The aspirant can become conversant in certain higher energies of consciousness in this way.

The Christian disciple would attempt to imitate Jesus Christ, hopefully discovering a little of what it feels like to be a Christ being. He or she could study the patriarchs of the Old Testament and attempt to walk in the consciousness they must have lived in or study Jesus' twelve disciples and walk in the consciousness of each. The feminine aspects are available by embracing the consciousness and purity of Jesus' mother, Mary, or studying and role-playing the consciousness of other significant women in the Bible. Each disciple should role-play both male and female archetypes in order to touch a balance of Christ qualities.

I have gained a lot from adapting this technique. One approach that worked for me is to role-play Jesus' thoughts. I gathered what I call Jesus' "power statements." For example: "I am the light of the world," "He who has seen me has seen the Father" (RSV), or "The Father and I are one" (NRSV).

I imagine myself as Jesus Christ and try to feel what it must be like to live in an expanded consciousness in which I could speak these statements with absolute sincerity. I would repeat one of Jesus' statements thousands of times. In each instance, I would stretch to feel more of the consciousness that could say this. This type of practice has been powerful in lifting my consciousness over a hump.

The process of role-playing or imitating Christ consciousness is extremely adaptable. You can probably find a way to incorporate it into your training program.

I have presented a number of patterns for creating your own practices. These are just for backup. There are an infinite number of approaches, and you will discover your own favorites.

It takes only one good spiritual practice to ferry you from hither to yon. As you can see, there are always at least a dozen sitting right in front of you. Brainstorm all manner of spiritual vehicles. Try them and choose one or several that feel promising. Then stick with them until you get results or evolve to further practices.

There is no magic formula for achieving a spiritual breakthrough. Simply trust yourself. You are a child of God. Within yourself you will find everything you need to express your divine heritage.

Chapter 7

GROUP WORK

Have you ever noticed that great people often come in clusters? Years ago I remember being amazed that different individuals who had a distinct impact upon the era in which they lived knew one another even if their talents lay in completely different areas.

My first conclusion was that famous people tend to meet other famous people because they share a common bond of notoriety. I'm sure that does happen. Yet in so many cases the individuals who have become trailblazers in their respective fields have known one another before they became famous.

With so few people in this world stepping out beyond the norm, doesn't it seem strange that several within a small circle of friends would make notable contributions in their respective fields? Wouldn't the law of equilibrium suggest that outstanding achievers be equally distributed among the masses?

My conclusion is that exceptional people *do* share a common bond. Fame is a by-product, not the cause of that bond. Each shares a deep appreciation for the creative spark that can carry one beyond the horizon. This spark can be channeled into philosophy, literature, science, statesmanship, art, music, or

117

spiritual development. Yet the experience of "plugging in" to a higher energy is much the same. Those who have entered that intense energy state tend to recognize and appreciate it in one another. One need not understand the particular task at which a friend excels in order to grasp, admire, and support the creative process by which it takes place.

Emerson and Thoreau were part of a circle of friends who blew on one another's creative spark. The founders of the United States of America were men of very different talents and backgrounds; yet by bouncing ideas off one another they created an idea bigger than any one of them.

How many would-be contributors to the progress of humanity have fallen along the way? Going it alone, their creative drive finally succumbed to the disappointments and frustrations of living alone on the frontiers of consciousness. The creative spark lights the tinder only when it is sheltered in loving hands and blown on gently for a time.

In many cases, this is achieved by a few friends cherishing and supporting the fragile forward steps each is making. When one begins to doubt himself or herself, the compatriot declares: "I see it and it's beautiful. Keep going!" When another is at a loss as to the next step, even a partner ignorant of the territory can brainstorm in a consciousness of incubation and the explorer gets that flash of light.

Thus great men and women have often evolved in groups. Even if the breakthroughs of only one or two were recognized with fame, all were great. The men and women shared consciousness. They blew on the flame. A fire erupted, burned out of control, and changed humanity.

If you are committed to spiritual exploration, establishing group consciousness will be very important to you. There are things a group can do that a single individual cannot. That is why we form marriage relationships, family units, hobby groups, churches, and companies. Gathered consciousness is often required for the big tasks of life. The spiritual trailblazer can benefit greatly from group support even though each path may seem unique.

Creating a group requires real finesse to be successful. It is easier to create a gathering that flies apart or scatters energy than to create one that focuses and empowers its participants.

For success, a group's purpose must be clearly understood and wisdom used in choosing partners. Structure needs to be established that supports focus and does not have a tendency to become sidetracked. Members must grasp group dynamics and understand the challenges of the laws of consciousness when applied to high-level support groups. In the end, few gatherings have solidified on these higher levels.

This is changing. We are entering an era in which we are beginning to master the art of merging higher consciousness for the benefit of the individual and the whole at the same time.

FRED

I first met Fred when I conducted his wedding. My wedding fee was the cheapest in town, and he was looking for a deal. While making arrangements for the wedding, he had requested a certain piece of classical music to be played for the recessional. However, he mischievously suggested, "I want it played well, and I'm the best pianist I know!" We all laughed at the joke. I found it even more amusing when, in the end, he recorded it, and we used the tape in the ceremony.

After the limo took Fred and his bride away, I didn't see him again for two years. Once contact was reestablished, our relationship evolved over several more years—from interesting acquaintance to respected friend. Ultimately, the bond became that of brothers sharing absolute admiration for the other's talent and potential.

Fred had creative talents in music that left me in absolute awe. He was an outstanding performer who could conduct feats of magic and absolute beauty in improvisation, composition, lyrics, and music production. He could move people with his music, and I wholeheartedly believed in him.

On the other hand, Fred admired my philosophical and spiritual perceptions; my ability to clarify, articulate, write, and teach; and my ability to touch others' lives through these mediums. He had absolute confidence in me. Together, we were more excited about the other's potentials and breakthroughs than our own.

We each had a deep spiritual life and confided our experiences, but more than anything, we shared an understanding of that high-voltage experience of channeling creative flow. One day he described his physical and mental responses when the spirit of composition would take command of him. I knew exactly what he felt. For me, it came during intense hours of writing, preparing a class, designing a program of spiritual activities, or creatively maneuvering people toward facing their problems.

A higher force takes over. Our nine-volt circuits are suddenly conducting a 220-volt flow. It's a thrill, but it wears on the system. Fred and I discussed adapting to the higher voltage in order to mature our talents. The sharing seemed to encourage that maturation in each of us.

There was no structure to our meetings. We would get together socially to talk, eat, and play. Always, conversation would revert back to our individual creative projects. I'd discuss my current realizations and read my latest written effort. He'd discuss lyrics to his new song and play whatever project he'd been working on in the studio.

With no real knowledge of music, I would praise and then critique his efforts. He would brainstorm with me as if I knew what I was talking about and would draw from our conversation improvements to his work. I would have no idea what I said that had helped to inspire him.

His comments on my latest realizations would add whole new aspects I hadn't considered. His side remarks and candid advice would focus me on major improvements to the approaches I would take.

He would rarely do what I suggested but gave me credit for the changes he chose to make. I rarely followed the exact approach he presented to me but depended upon him for the inspiration that did evolve. The gift we had for each other was not expertise. It was a high-energy state that we shared when we gathered. We each thrived in the creative, supportive environment our bond was built upon. This was my deepest experience of what a "creativity cell" could be.

The cell was actually a little larger. Fred's wife Merrilee ended up working closely with both Fred and me on our projects and drove us, unmercifully, toward our dreams. When I finally married, my wife Karrin added a whole new energy of support to the group.

When any of us would get discouraged or lazy about pursuing our dreams, the gathering would inspire us and get us moving again. Merrilee and Karrin discussed with the group where they could express their particular creative drives, beyond just being supportive of Fred's music or my teaching.

Ultimately, every one of us was carried forward by the wave our gathering generated.

CREATIVITY CELL

A *creativity cell* is a gathering of a few people (from two to six or eight) whose purpose is to support one another in expressing that higher energy through whatever medium comes most naturally. The members of a cell can share similar talents or have entirely different expertise and aspirations. It works both ways.

A creativity cell based on the desire for spiritual exploration can provide tremendous assistance in gaining and retaining a foothold in the frontier. The individual spiritual projects may be quite different, but sharing is always inspiring. Furthermore, when the group has faith in you, there is more purpose to hanging tough through the discouraging times.

The key to the successful spiritual exploration "creativity cell" is gathering in the correct consciousness. Members are not there to tell one another how to do anything or show how far they've come. They are there to believe in one another and to set aside ego, competition, and personal opinion and support one another in their particular projects.

They gather to regain the forward impetus that allows the high-voltage, creative experience to happen. They will share with compatriots sensitive, delicate experiences which could lead to breakthroughs and will know that they will receive only support. Critique is handled as brainstorming, not criticism. Partners on the quest need to be honest, sincere, interested individuals ready to offer honest thoughts. Above all, each member's job is to make fellow members aware of their exquisite potential and keep them on the path toward their dreams.

Small prayer groups have become very popular, probably because they have proven to be truly powerful. They employ similar structure and bonding but are aimed at a different mark. I encourage you to participate in a small, personal prayer group, but the explorer needs a "creativity cell" too.

If your prayer partners decide to expand to include exploration-group goals, keep the two functions segmented so that clear purpose can be maintained for both aspects. In a prayer group, the members pray for one another. They don't discuss or advise. They pray. In a creativity cell, members share, brainstorm, and encourage one another.

The same people can fulfill both functions as long as they understand clearly what each function is. You can pray then break from the prayer time to discuss exploration projects, but not to advise in the prayer request. Another approach would be to conduct the different functions at different times.

The many support groups available in our society are full of advice-giving and emotional dumping. They aim at bonding through sharing gut-level experiences. This is wonderful for those who need this kind of support, but it relies upon a lower-level emotional connection.

A support group for individuals reaching into the spiritual frontier depends upon merging at the highest levels of consciousness. If the group degenerates into an emotional dumping ground, its ability to keep you in touch with the high voltage energy is lost.

ADVANCED BREATHWORK

Several years back, Karrin and I gathered with five or six others to explore the use of an advanced technique of intense breathwork that originated with Stanislav and Christina Grof.

We hoped to use the technique as a tool for reaching higher spiritual experiences.

The facilitators of this particular breathwork style used music, essences, affirmation, sound in many forms, touch, bodywork, energy work, chakra work, and above all, their own breathing to assist the individual making the journey. They depended upon attuning themselves to the consciousness of the breather. They intuitively trusted a higher guidance to show them exactly how to help the breather break through points of spiritual blockage on the upward climb. The process was quite unusual, and there were few skilled facilitators.

Having had minimal exposure to this technique, we knew that none of us were truly qualified to facilitate such a venture. We determined that we would have to depend upon the merged consciousness of the group to provide the energy and skill each of us lacked individually. We would join in knowing that Spirit was guiding us. If we were one with one another and one with God, it was safe to make the journey.

We gathered, conversed quietly to unite the group energy, and prayed together in preparation. Then one person would lie down and the rest would gather around to facilitate. As a group, we would begin the breathwork and jump off into the unknown. Most sessions lasted an hour and a half to two hours. We met weekly for nine months.

EGO CLEANSING

The results were astounding. I had several of my most powerful spiritual experiences with this group. However, there was a price. Uniting in consciousness at this high level required a purification of individual egos in order for the group to merge at the higher level. After all, ego is defined by individual separateness. Group consciousness is accomplished by removing the boundaries and functioning as one.

The first of the challenges to emerge was control. Different facilitators would head in different directions. There is a delicate balance between being true to the inspiration you feel within yourself and allowing for a different inspiration within one of your mates that is just as valid or even more appropriate at the time.

For things to go well, the group had to remain harmoniously balanced with no one person controlling the direction. We discovered that each of us had different talents. If there was confusion as to what to do, we would defer to the one who excelled in that particular area.

Thus we learned to work as a team. But no one's contribution in any area was considered inferior. Spirit could move through any one of us. There was beauty in the way the group created an experience that was far above anything any one of us individually could have hoped for. It was inspiring to see how high we could go as a group once we mastered the ego-control issues and learned to truly function as one.

On the other hand, there were continual ego-cleansing requirements the farther we went. Issues between husband and wife surfaced. Issues between different individuals erupted. Each time, we dealt with them, released them for the good of the whole, allowed love to replace them, and gained new height.

We encountered ego bruising, the tendency toward criticism or condemnation, the need to elevate oneself to the status of expert, competition, subtle power struggles, the fantasy of being too spiritually evolved for ego problems (better known as denial), unwillingness to open fully to the group, and even jealousy. This sounds like a dreadful list but the expressions of these issues and activities were quite subtle. They could easily have been missed in other groups. They were magnified by the height to which we aspired.

We honestly faced and removed our unexpected warts in order to return our attention to the real purpose for our gathering. Each time we did, we were admitted to a higher level of group consciousness.

After nine months of releasing these subtle adversaries and rising to a new level of love and trust, group consciousness reached an intense level. In these higher realms of bonding, a small ego issue can create havoc. There can be no holding back. One issue arose that we tried to ignore, and the group fell apart.

Ego cleansing for the purpose of merging consciousness is a very small part of the experience an exploration group will encounter, but it cannot be ignored. It is the ticket price for admission to the main attraction. Pretend you are too spiritual for any of these warts and your group will never soar. Face your small ego sacrifices honestly and the power of the group will astound you.

However, there is a balance to be maintained. Concentrate too much on removal of imperfections and you degenerate into an emotional support group. You'll never gain the heights. Honestly face your shortcomings as they arise, let love replace them, and quickly move on to your main agenda.

SMALL EXPLORATION GROUPS

Your main agenda is the intense spiritual work only a small cell of dedicated partners can sustain. Regular contact with these few who share your inner world will push you forward when you need it most.

The power generated in the small cell is almost addictive, but there are other levels of group work that a larger, more diverse gathering provides. Cells need to network with other cells to keep their horizons broadened. Members within a certain intimate group will each have connections with others in different areas or on different levels. In this way, no single group becomes an island. Each cell is connected to other cells through its individual members. Soon the structure looks like a huge honeycomb and there is a subtle strength gained from being part of the larger structure. The small cell that jealously isolates itself from the larger whole loses something important. After all, the flow of spiritual awakening is toward oneness with the whole.

Ego (the need to hold separation) is faced on a new level in the small group. The individual has to give up a degree of isolation to merge in consciousness with this group of a few. The few must give up their natural tendency toward isolating their newfound, high-level intimacy to protect it. Small-group pride and privacy must be sacrificed to participate in merging on a larger scale. Each step brings expanded challenges and expanded rewards.

Spiritual exploration is a large arena. Any group gathered under this banner will span a generous range of ideals, dedication, perspectives, and energy levels.

LARGER EXPLORATION GROUPS

The larger spiritual exploration group will have challenges, without a doubt. Its expanded size makes it harder to sustain a constructive direction and to keep on task. It will severely test love, acceptance, and openness in regard to personal inner experiences. Fear of rejection increases, barriers take longer to fall, and trust takes longer to establish.

Yet the larger gathering embodies an exciting diversity of experience that expands horizons. Once in motion, it carries quite a sense of synergy for the individual to draw upon.

Sometimes it is better to create the larger spiritual exploration group first. Those drawn to the basic idea of exploring the frontier of our higher potential come together and begin to share. Members have a large pool from which to select their intimate circle of partners. Shortly those with similar objectives or energy levels are drawn together. They work together and periodically present their findings to the larger group.

Within the large group, cells may develop for intense, experiential excursions into practicing healing work, developing intuition, experiencing God in the silence, doing dreamwork, moving invisible energies, connecting to the Source of all abundance, extending mind capabilities, mastering prayer, reaching out to the angelic kingdom, merging with nature, following divine guidance, and so forth. The real work will take place in the intimate circle of those directed to a particular project. As each cell shares its results, the members of the group at large receive treasures from areas in which they haven't worked.

I was a part of a gathering of around thirty people who flocked to the ideal of spiritual exploration. From the beginning, we determined that a group this large would have to depend upon structure to keep on the right track. It is too easy for thirty people to pull in thirty different directions and go nowhere. A few can talk everything out as diverging desires arise. Thirty cannot.

The first few meetings were dedicated to outlining a structure that would keep us on course. What were the rules of our encounters? Were there times when we were going to have no rules?

STRUCTURE SUGGESTIONS

The first topic of structure was whether meetings would be open to newcomers each week or closed to new participants once the group began. The open format provides a constant flow of new energy. It also allows new people not committed to the ideal of spiritual exploration to come watch the show. They could leave and talk of how bizarre the whole thing was. The frontier is often bizarre.

We felt that would inhibit open sharing when new faces joined those of the trusted gathering. Thus we opted for a closed group which *periodically* opened to new members.

A rule was established that no one could be verbally attacked in regard to what he or she shared. This was to be a safe environment. Debate was discouraged, though members were expected to present differing views, discuss, and question those sharing.

The assembly of "explorers" was quite diversified. In one meeting, Sheryl was describing an experience that she'd had for years but had never told anyone about. She described a certain state of consciousness in which she perceived little bits of energy in the air. They seemed almost alive. As she would move through them with thought energy, they would swirl as if physically disturbed by the invisible movement of her thought. Then she asked, "Has anyone else had this experience?"

The responses were mixed. A few conceded they had experienced similar phenomena though had never thought to describe it in that way. With consternation on their faces, some asked questions to clarify. Finally, Ray spoke up and said, "Am I the only one here who thinks she's bonkers?" Everyone laughed.

Honest and direct as his response was, there was no breech of trust. We had built a consciousness of loving acceptance in our gatherings. It was not a rejection to say, "I'm sorry; I can't go that far with you." After all, others may find out that their experience is imagined or "bonkers." Alternately, they may discover that they have touched the seeds of something big. In either case, it takes exploration to find out. That's why we gather.

Unwieldy as it may be, the large-group experience has a lot to offer. It is naive to assume that members will share their work each week as they would in the small cells. The larger gatherings should be designed to accentuate the strength gained from numbers. This gathering might be less frequent than the weekly schedule for the smaller work groups.

The meeting structure might include an opening prayer, followed by a sharing time: "Has anyone had a breakthrough experience to report this week?" The main program would occupy the bulk of the allotted time. The meeting would end with a ritual closing circle.

MEETING APPROACHES

The main body of the meeting could take many forms. The most obvious would be project presentations by the different cells within the large group. Eventually, the small cells should volunteer to spend a meeting sharing what they have done, what has worked, and what has not. Little successes are exciting to hear about. Techniques or conclusions from a small group could be adapted by other groups or by the large group. One of the main objectives is to share the fruits of everyone's labor.

Within the group I attended, we had presentations on telepathy, tapping intuition, different aspects of healing, angelic encounters, and awakening the heart center, to name a few. Each presenting cell not only would tell of efforts and results but also would devise practices and meditations that would enable the whole group to get a taste of the experience.

One individual experienced literal prophetic dreaming on a fairly regular basis. She agreed to watch herself closely and keep detailed records of everything that surrounded these events. Though it flowed naturally for her, she analyzed and dissected all the feelings and happenings surrounding these spectacular dreams in preparation for her presentation. Eventually, she shared everything she could and answered a barrage of questions, allowing others to find a foothold toward a similar experience.

A slightly different approach to meeting was "path-sharing" night. One individual would spin the tale of spiritual awakening in his or her life. These evenings were captivating. Each saga proved rich in lessons for everyone. We would return to our own spiritual journey with renewed enthusiasm.

"Topic night" consisted of picking a subject and encouraging members to share any experience they had encountered in the territory. I remember a particularly inspiring evening in which members shared their most dramatic experiences with dreams. We covered the entire span of dreamwork from simple symbolic guidance to lucid dreaming.

However, the most exciting topic night was on Christ encounters: "Share any experience, dramatic or very subtle, in which you realized a higher Self existed inside of you." This night we went around the circle, one by one. The session took a long time but kept our attention.

Some gatherings should be dedicated to spiritual experience that only a group can create. Declare a "praise" or "gratefulness" evening. The main body of the meeting is designated for concentrating only upon these uplifting qualities for the normal meeting time.

The objective is to verbalize your gratitude around the circle without ceasing for forty-five minutes or an hour. The group may respond and repeat as a whole each statement each individual makes.

By the end, the energies are intense. A time should be taken to silently identify the higher energy state and integrate it into your consciousness. Remind the others to assess the changes this energy level stimulated in their lives after leaving the meeting.

A gathering can be dedicated to chanting for an evening. Even further, one session might be charted for silence. Sit together in silence until the closing prayer. The effect can be riveting.

RITUALS

Within the larger group, ritual plays the role of tying everything together. It doesn't take much, but a group should be able to depend upon certain regimens to create a regular vehicle for merging consciousness and keeping the meeting on purpose.

You may want to devise your own little ceremonies for opening and closing. One group opened with a prayer led by a different person each time. They then closed by gathering in a circle holding hands. A lighted candle was silently passed from person to person around the circle. As one individual passed it to the next, he or she would look in the other's eyes and quietly affirm: *I behold the Christ in you.* This ended every meeting with sacredness. It reminded all why we gather—to support one another by seeing the highest within each one.

Accepting new members can be another repeated ritual. Treat it as a sacred initiation. Recap the original ideals that brought the group together. This draws longtime members back on target while indoctrinating new ones. Devise a simple ceremony that marks the initiation.

Create whatever rituals or ceremonies you like to remind everyone at each meeting of the group's sacred mission. When used regularly, these short little rituals grow dear to everyone's heart. They become much-needed anchors.

CHALLENGES

All expanded groups meet their challenges. Members must be reminded of the necessity for confidentiality in regard to what is shared. Trust can be destroyed by careless words.

On one hand, discipline must be maintained to keep the group from degenerating into a debate or an intellectual discussion group. On the other hand, the group that degenerates into pure "touchy-feely" experience or a subtle competition for the wildest experience of the week is equally off base.

There must be a balance of pure spiritual experience and intellectual analysis in order to create a body of mind-and-heart understanding that can be our legacy to those who follow.

The most destructive pitfall I've seen is allowing the group to become a "sampling group" instead of a "spiritual work group." The group degenerates into sampling when the members get lazy about reporting their practices and results (or lack of them).

Sharing progress implies that each individual is spending serious time on spiritual practices each week. His or her report may be mundane. "I've been working with this practice, but I can't seem to break through." Or, "I think something's beginning to happen, but I'm not sure." This kind of sharing may not seem very exciting, but it is real. Group support can lead this person to a real breakthrough. That's exciting!

No one expects you to be a spiritual adept overnight. If you begin to sound like one, examine whether your desire for quick results is pushing you into fantasy.

When the members aren't doing their homework or they are embarrassed to report that they are inching along, the group heads for sampling. They try something new each week and never experience anything at great depth. The meeting becomes entertainment, not the fulfillment of spiritual purpose. Shortly people will be suggesting getting outside speakers to keep the program interesting.

The main objective of believing in one another and pooling experiences is lost. Attendance drops off. Consciousness is scattered. The group disintegrates.

Don't get me wrong. A sampling meeting has its place and is a lot of fun to attend. It just doesn't serve the deeply sacred purpose of those aspiring to become part of the spiritual vanguard. Focused intent is the most powerful tool at the group's disposal. Betray your mystical intent and there is no energy to hold the group together.

Attrition is normal. Not all are as committed to hard spiritual work as they think. Those who drop off strengthen your group consciousness by leaving only those with enduring commitment.

Avoid the pitfalls, grow through the challenges, and your group (whatever its size) will serve you well. Group consciousness is powerful beyond our expectations. Yet it is a relatively unexplored territory. We are only beginning to tap this experience.

In the years ahead, we will develop and refine the art of gathering. This art of merging with one another will open the higher realms to us. We will begin to wield energies and work in realms that no *separate* being can attain. The possibilities are thrilling. It might even be this frontier of group consciousness itself that you will use your life to explore.

Chapter 8

CREATING THE PROTOTYPE

A friend of mine, Joyce, was the executive assistant to the project manager in charge of creating a viable solar generator to be used to power a normal household. Her boss had brain-stormed a unit using available cutting-edge technology combined with some new concepts of his own.

After designing the entire unit on paper, the parent company agreed the design had real possibilities. The company gave the project the funding necessary to create a prototype. A working model was needed to determine how to mass-produce these units.

This first model was painstakingly created with each little problem that arose solved at each stage of development.

It took the form of a 16-foot-diameter ball constructed in geodesic-dome style combined with a parabolic reflector. The reflector used a tracking device to move it throughout the day so that it constantly concentrated the sun's rays through a thick quartz window into the center of the ball.

The 16-foot ball was heavily insulated and held a certain alloy of metal that would melt under the high heat conveyed by the parabolic reflector. The alloy would hold this heat and slowly release it as the metal returned from liquid to solid

137

form. Thus it stored and released the sun's heat energy over a period of time.

The project manager personally held five patents on the prototype, a couple of which related to the special combination of metals that produced the most efficient results for storing and releasing heat.

The heat slowly released was harnessed to run a small steam turbine that could produce enough electricity to run a normal household.

Once the prototype was completed, the testing began. The unit proved quite successful at generating the necessary electricity. Surprisingly enough, it proved equally successful at storing the heat. Once fully activated, the molten metallic solution was capable of releasing its heat slowly enough to continue to power its generator for up to thirty consecutive cloudy days. Though large and unwieldy, the prototype operated exceptionally well.

The only drawback was cost. The prototype had cost $200,000. However, the project manager believed that with improvements and mass production, the price could be cut to a tenth or a twentieth of what it cost to build the prototype. He was working on design refinements and brainstorming smaller units that could be adapted to other uses, like powering cars, when all the funding got pulled, and the project was abandoned. Joyce and her boss found themselves unemployed.

It seems that a large conglomerate with an emphasis on products involved in the current production of mass electricity had acquired the parent company. Shortly those in charge of company profits decided that this project did not warrant the financial support it needed to go forward. It was ordered abandoned.

A SPIRITUAL PROTOTYPE

I tell this story because if you are drawn to the spiritual exploration of the "inner core," you are part of a research group dedicated to creating a prototype of the spiritual potential for the next millennium. You are willing to use your life to develop a spiritual potential that (imperfect as your working model may be) will be refined and absorbed almost effortlessly by whole generations that will follow.

The challenges of the prototype are the same in spiritual realms as they are in technical development. A real spiritual breakthrough, like its technological counterpart, will be costly. It will require extensive time and effort and the dedication of the most valuable commodity we have to offer—our lifetime. It takes a lot of ingenuity, tenacity, and patience to create the first of anything.

Using currently available cutting-edge concepts and some of our own ingenuity, we will awaken and harness spiritual energies only fantasized about thus far. Each small step will seem tedious and present problems to be solved. Finally, with the awakening of a new spiritual potential, we enter the testing phase. We must explore the limits of our working model.

The enemy of serious spiritual breakthrough is the same one encountered by our friends pioneering in solar energy. The needs of the "status quo" can be so demanding as to choke off the time and energy necessary to create break-through. When the world floods our life with an array of pressing demands, it cuts our funding for the advanced prototype project.

Our job is to beat the odds—to defy the sleep that defends our human nature against the onslaught of our divine nature. It is time for the slave of physical limitation to become its master. But do not believe this role reversal will come without pain. The world as we know it will resist. Human limitation will savagely defend its authority. Spiritual freedom and our divine inheritance will be won with unyielding commitment and endurance each step of the journey.

Changing the whole way humanity relates to the Earth will not be easy. Just changing the level at which a few of us interact with our earthly lives will consume all the energy we have to give. Results may be slow in coming. What small freedoms we can gain may seem to come at a high price. But we came into this life to sail the transition from one age of human expression into another. Spiritual freedom is the only gift we can offer our children and our children's children.

In 1975 I attended a show at the Miami Planetarium that followed the stars through the evolution of human beings on this planet. We entered the domed auditorium and leaned back in our chairs to gaze at the ceiling; someone dimmed the lights. At the flip of a switch, a technician powered up a huge complicated machine that cast laser-projected stars onto a night sky above us.

The creators of this show had projected the flow of the stars back through history and prehistory to give us the clear vision of a night sky at the dawn of humanity. The presentation progressed by moving the stars forward to show us a typical night sky at the advent of each new subspecies of humankind.

The narrator described the evolution of the human species, progressing through Homo erectus, Neanderthal man, Cro-Magnon man, and other subspecies along the way to modern man, Homo sapiens. We hit a few night skies during critical times along the journey of modern man. The show seemed to climax with an extensive description of the night sky of the present day accompanied by a description of the new awareness and technological breakthroughs accomplished by modern man.

Just when we thought it was over, the narrator took us a step further, projecting the stars into the future—the next millennium. He began to outline the new dramatic breakthroughs in inner energies that would change the whole way the species functions in this world. He suggested that new powers were beginning to emerge within the human mind.

A NEW SPECIES

With the increase of psychic phenomena, telepathy, precognition, telekinesis, and even the power of prayer on plants, the narrator submitted that we were at the crest of another major unexplained leap forward in human consciousness. The human experience was entering into new awareness and new potentials that could elevate the expression of the species so far above modern man's perceptions, as to equal the leap from Neanderthal man to modern man.

The show ended with the narrator's declaring that we may well be living during an era when the Homo sapiens species is metamorphosing into something greater. Possibly the leap covers so much territory as to warrant a new label, "Homo illuminous."

This planetarium show has stuck in my memory all of

these years because I believe that it captured the true excitement of the era in which we live. The technological revolution, the information society, all the new electronic toys, even the advent of space travel are small stakes compared to the new frontier dawning on humankind from within.

Spiritual exploration is not about a few people getting ahead by tapping higher energies within. It's not about personal advancement. It's about the whole human species and our appointment with a higher destiny.

We are the vanguard of a new human species. An example was given to us by Jesus Christ. It has been fixed into our race consciousness during the last two millennia. The seed has germinated. The desire has been sown into our hearts. Our job is to push that first sprout through the hard-packed soil of human life as we have known it.

We will likely not see the beauty of the plant reaching blossom while in our present physical bodies. Under the direction of Jesus Christ and all the great beings of Light that caretake this planet, we have the privilege of sprouting the awareness of the new human consciousness, a consciousness of divine Sonship and Daughtership. The real glory of what we help to spawn will probably not mature for several generations to come. We have the privilege of hearing and answering a call extended to all humanity everywhere. Our meager efforts will be our gift to human history.

Two thousand years ago, the Christ entered the Earth and the consciousness of Homo sapiens as one powerful, fully awakened Son of God we know as Jesus Christ. Jesus not only entered Christ consciousness, he merged with Sonship and became "the Christ."

Much of Homo sapiens patiently awaits the return of

that one great being to physical form. The limited vision of Homo sapiens fails to see that Jesus never left. He merely ascended into the higher energy levels that permeate the planet. Awakening Homo illuminous is beginning to see these higher dimensions and recognizes that the second coming of Christ has already begun. It is the awakening of Christ within the minds and hearts of every human being upon the planet.

The vision of the golden age is of a planet transformed into a garden of beauty by application of higher energies. All humanity will live in the higher realms where Jesus did his miracles, and humanity's presence here becomes a blessing to all earthly life. The vision is that of a world filled with Christ beings, sons and daughters of God, celebrating the glory of Earth's primitive beauty.

We who answer the call of our soul will strive toward the higher dimensions. We will make hard-earned breakthroughs for ourselves and for humanity. But we will not be the final product of the spiritual revolution. We will be "the beginning."

Humanity's greatest accomplishments often took the cooperation of individuals who could embrace an ideal whose fruition was larger than their own lifetimes. One generation would commence building an ancient temple and be unable to finish it. A later generation would complete and live in it.

When we dedicate our lives to creating the prototype, we give them to those dear generations who will follow us. Our breakthroughs will thrill us. But we are the beginning.

We will crack the door to the kingdom. In time, our joy will be made full by watching from a higher dimension as future residents of the Earth (who, in the end, are one with us) walk in and dwell in the kingdom of God expressed in the Earth.

Visions this lofty and far-reaching often leave us feeling small and inadequate. So let's bring it back to the mission at hand. How can we facilitate spiritual awakening? If Homo illuminous is calling, how can we begin to answer?

I admire Charles Fillmore for his exploration into the higher mystical realms. In his book *Atom-Smashing Power of Mind*, he brings the whole task down to earth with the statement: "We must not anticipate better social and economic conditions until we have better men and women to institute and sustain those conditions" (p. 31).

In the last era of humankind, we set out to master the world, to adapt it to better fit our needs. Technology has become king. Using the brilliance of these God-given minds, we have learned the secrets of the physical world and turned them back upon the Earth itself. We have harnessed the very forces that provided our obstacles.

Technology is a wonderful excursion into understanding and harmonizing with the primitive forces that constitute the Earth. Yet, with all our mastery of nature, we still live in a world where there is starvation, injustice, unhappiness in the midst of opulence, competition, the struggle for personal power, success of the strongest, and failure of others. Brutal suffering and subtle suffering are still part of the human experience. So far, technology can't feed the world, stop an earthquake or a hurricane, or provide the people of the Earth with true happiness.

Maybe it could accomplish a couple of these tasks if it were profitable enough for those who have the power to direct our resources in that direction. The problem is not with technology. It is with the Homo sapiens who wield it. Until we have better people, we will never deserve a better world, and we always get the world we, as a whole, deserve.

We need to create an advanced human race so that technology can harmonize with higher forces and serve a nobler master. An advanced race is grown one being at a time. This is how we change the world for the better.

Utopias fall apart because of their people. Become the prototype of the advanced human being, and Heaven on Earth is finally a possibility. The inner must come first. The outer will follow. It is spiritual exploration that holds the key to our future and to all of our dreams.

It is often easier to keep on track if we can see the overall plan. Let's for a moment look at the basic ground we must cover to become part of the developing prototype.

There are three basic areas to be developed. First, we must build a strong spiritual foundation. This is our intimate relationship with and our experience of God. Without this, all mind powers are sleight of hand.

Second, we must incorporate the use of higher energies and expanded perspectives into our daily activities. Third, we must push the envelope, strive for true higher-level experiences that are beyond the present evolution of human consciousness. Many of these transcendent experiences have physical counterparts that society would call miracles.

A STRONG SPIRITUAL FOUNDATION

Jesus began his ministry with forty days of retreat in the wilderness. Whenever I am getting serious about spiritual expansion, I kick off my efforts with some form of retreat. I believe you will find it useful too.

If you want to speak with power, spend time in silence. If you want to understand the higher energies of sexual exchange, go celibate for a time with that intention. If you want to experience the magical higher energies that fill the air at Christmas, spend one alone—just you and the spirit of Christmas. If you want to dedicate your life to becoming a living example of higher human potential, withdraw and go into the privacy of your innermost, unearthly consciousness to make your agreements and claim your power.

Nothing centers us and sets us on our way like a vacation from outer demands, outer distractions, and outer entertainment. Whenever the journey toward the prototype bogs down, retreat momentarily to once again find that sense of power which propels us forward. Retreat, gather power, leap forward.

INCORPORATE EXPANSION INTO DAILY ACTIVITIES

Retreat can often kick off a leap into higher-energy experience, but the real work remains. We must maintain the high-level experience and integrate it into our daily lives. We accomplish this through tenacious use of spiritual practices, concentration on the higher potential (almost to the point of obsession), meditation, prayer, and the channeling of this spiritual energy into mundane activities.

Some will say: "You're trying too hard! Simply enjoy your life, and God will teach you all along the way." I agree, but that's only half the story.

Life is a school, without a doubt. As with all schools of higher education, there is the required course of study and then there are the electives for those who want to study further.

We all take the required course. Only the dedicated ones take the electives. They require a conscious choice.

God's required course is wonderful. It adapts itself to the needs of each soul. We can cover the material at our own rate. As we pay attention and learn from what life sends our way, illumination dawns in so many different areas. Ignore life's messages and the program plods along. Pay attention and the mile markers start to fly by.

Much of spiritual training is presently aimed at the required course of study, urging us to look for the gifts the teacher (the Holy Spirit) leaves for us at every turn. We learn and grow through life, sometimes at quite a demanding rate. Our corners get knocked off. We learn to embrace change daily. Spirit seems to be dragging us toward our destiny of Homo illuminous. The required course is the most dynamic force in our spiritual lives. As we learn to embrace it, we are amazed at how deftly God is molding us.

PUSH THE ENVELOPE

Those who pay attention to the required course of study that God has placed in front of us at all times go to the head of the class. Yet real spiritual pioneers don't settle for just immersing themselves in the required program. They ask for more. They take an elective by asking for an assignment, setting their sights on this higher potential, allowing their lives to become a laboratory, and doing whatever it takes to break through the walls that hold them back. Spiritual explorers hammer away at an elective at the same time that they are embracing whatever spiritual lesson life is requiring of them.

At one point, my path required that I learn humility. For several years it seemed that I was learning to "accept the unacceptable." I've come to believe that many higher-realm lessons involve this surrender to God—humility.

This is classic required course. It rocks our very foundation. The experiences we endure sculpt personality. We change dramatically and sometimes are even crushed into submission. All is accomplished in order to create channels in our consciousness that are capable of transmitting God-awareness. In the end, we do it to ourselves. God does not beat us into submission, though it may feel that way. To succeed is often simply to endure to the point of surrender.

In speaking with a friend about this period in my life, I declared: "I am very willful. I'm used to winning. After years of struggle, I lost the battle. I simply surrendered. And thank God I did. Thank God I lost. The freedom that came to me from this surrender has changed my life more than anything for many years."

She responded, "Yes, I've been humiliated over and over in the last few months." She faltered and corrected, "I mean humbled."

I instantly retorted: "The word *humiliated* indicates how deeply you are still immersed in the battle. Only one who has not yet surrendered can be humiliated. This emotion does not exist for one who has surrendered to God. Humbleness is a strength—a freedom from any possibility of humiliation. Of course I spent years resisting surrender. You will travel the path much more quickly, I am sure."

The required course enables us to *be* a son or daughter of God. The electives involve learning to wield the powers of which a son or daughter has custody.

While plumbing the depths of humility (or at least one level of it), I found my attention was drawn over and over to healing. This is the way an elective is offered. The required course of the day was personality surrender, but I took the cue and started pursuing healing life at the same time.

My affirmation became: *I want to learn to heal myself and others.* I figured as a son of God I had the right to experience and channel awareness of God's healing life into specific situations.

The elective courses are often centered upon "doing" something with the divine inheritance. Here we awaken and train the spiritual muscles that will wield this "power" which is entrusted to a son or a daughter of God. It will eventually become a part of the required course, but it is offered a number of times earlier on the path for those who have the initiative to pursue it.

Spiritual explorers are those who push the envelope of divine expression ("doing") at each stage of development. The explorer's lone breakthrough has far-reaching results. The same breakthrough begins to creep up around the globe. Before long it is absorbed effortlessly into mass consciousness.

Jesus declared, "I, if I be lifted up from the earth, will draw all men unto me." I keep returning to this. There is no clearer statement of purpose for anyone who dedicates his or her life to becoming the prototype of a higher evolution of humankind—sons and daughters of God incarnate.

HUMAN EVOLUTION

Human evolution has always been driven by an advancement in the tools by which we master our world. Early caveman learned that a club was more powerful than a hand. Almost instantly, his fellows mastered the club or were vanquished. This was followed by the jump to the spear and then the bow. With each improvement, the old way of life disappeared. The law was "evolve or die."

The shovel and plow brought about the demise of the gathering cultures. Gunpowder shifted the balance of power again. Less technologically advanced cultures jumped to acquire and master the gun in order to avoid annihilation. Along the way, we learned that strategy could outweigh weapon power. Once again, humanity jumped forward. Get smart or die.

The modern age brought industry, advanced transportation, and communication. In a few years time-honored ways of life vanished, replaced by a technological society.

Today we scramble to become computer-literate in order to survive. Our children master the use of artificial intelligence by the second grade.

In a short hundred years, humanity has evolved from a worldwide horse-and-buggy society to jet travel and cell phones for everyone, even in third-world countries. Technology is king. We assume it will continue to rule into the foreseeable future.

Alas, I believe it will not. We stand at the edge of a precipice that will catapult us into a leap which will make technology look like puddle jumping. The only question that remains is who will leap first. After that, everyone else will have to follow like lemmings plunging into the sea.

The development of higher mind powers and the use of spiritual energies by God men and women will devastate society as we now know it.

Science fiction has already caught wind of the coming crisis. Stories abound pitting an emerging culture of telepaths against more limited human beings depending upon privacy, secrecy, and deception. Others hint at the dominance of elevated cultures in which all members consciously dip into the mind net.

They miss the mark only because science fiction tends to leave God out and keep human shortcomings intact. Very few realize that higher powers will be wielded by awakening God men and women, not by degraded egos with a bigger mental gun.

Nonetheless, I believe the world as we know it is headed toward cataclysm. Very few of our present societal structures will survive a leap from Homo sapiens to Homo illuminous. Economy, life priorities, the balance of power, production of goods and services, political structure, human values, and personal conflict resolution are all based on competition, individual inner separation, and physical limitations. When these change, our structures of society collapse.

Out of their ashes will rise higher structures based upon divine principles and divine power . . . "A new heaven and a new earth . . . and God himself shall be with them, and be their God." We will live in knowledge of the "oneness" of life instead of the belief in our separation.

HOMO ILLUMINOUS ARRIVES

It has begun. There is no avoiding this shift. We might just as easily hang on to our bows and arrows, hoping to stop the advance of an armored-tank division. Homo illuminous is arriving. Homo sapiens will disappear from the Earth. Our only choice is whether we shall fight against our destined higher good or embrace it openly and teach what we learn. In the latter case, we lend our energies to as smooth and painless a transition as is possible.

Let me explain how just one structure of society or economy will be forever altered by spiritual awakening. If you master divine guidance and are allowed access to Universal Mind on a regular basis, economy, as we presently know it, is at your mercy. As you learn to dip into Divine Mind to see what stock will rise tomorrow, the economic balance, based on lack of knowledge, is placed in jeopardy. As others learn this ability with you, everyone must make the jump or lose his or her financial fortune. When everyone can see what was previously invisible, the system no longer works. A higher system based on expanded parameters of human expression must replace it.

In the early years of transition, technology will embrace the new mental capabilities that surface. The power of machinery will be aimed upon the awakening infant of advanced brain-powers. Instrumentation will be used to stimulate energy awakenings and act as training grounds for those who will master these energies. Man and machine will be partnered. Thought will activate machines much as voice does already. Thought and emotion will be amplified with the attempt to harness them technologically.

The whole scientific foray will encourage extreme mental and emotional discipline by society as a whole. Mental and emotional training will be the way to get ahead, just as becoming computer-literate has been in this era.

The more the power of mind over matter is explored, the less dependent upon machinery the whole process will become. Technology will fade as mind power begins to stand on its own.

For a short time, individuals, governments, and corporations will attempt to harness mind-energy awakenings for old, selfish purposes based in that hard-to-die concept of individual separation from the whole.

However, within spiritual circles, advanced mind awakenings will be tethered to higher intent. Christ-centered men and women not only will master mental energies and harness them to the good of the whole, but they also will learn to dip into universal mind and universal power.

Touching the One and channeling God's power as a child of God will surpass individual higher mental power so far as to make it obsolete. This is why it is so important that we dedicate our lives to developing some aspect of the higher spiritual prototype. The more quickly we awaken this Christ prototype and learn to flex higher spiritual muscles whose source is God, the more swiftly this destructive side trip into individual higher mental energy guided by human limitation will pass. Humanity will be drawn up into Homo illuminous instead of getting stuck between the two evolutions.

A GOLDEN AGE

I foresee a golden age ahead, though I may not live to see it fully implemented. I see a future Earth inhabited by men and women who know they are sons and daughters of God and are our descendents. They will be born knowing, for that knowledge will be the gift of our human race consciousness.

In this coming world, we will not spend most of our lives trying to unlearn our limitations, overcome emotional garbage we have gathered, and reverse family patterns that seem to be passed through the genes. Today "clean up" is the path to spiritual awakening. In our future, fear based on belief in separation will not exist. Imagine being born from the beginning with a clean slate, remembrance of your spiritual origin, and the support and training to develop your full potential as a child of God.

Earth will be our garden. We will step lightly upon its breathtaking beauty. We will cherish it. The wind, the currents of the sea, the growth of plants, and the evolvement of animal life will all be forces that are our friends. Our presence here will bring harmony. Our own needs will be met spiritually and in the totally harmonious participation in the cycle of life. It will be a great joy to participate in the pageant of Earth, not subdue it with a slave-master relationship.

As survival becomes a nonissue because of our mastery of higher energy forces to meet our needs, creativity will become the economy of life, not money. The consciousness of oneness will allow us to leave no one's needs unfulfilled. Everyone will live in abundance, though the state of plenty will be measured in different ways. No longer will we measure our economic security by what we can hoard unto ourselves. Abundance will be shared by all. What beauty we individually cocreate with God will be the measure of our wealth, and sharing, the way we spend it.

Death will no longer be shrouded in darkness. It will be celebrated like birth. We will enter the Earth consciously and leave it consciously as well. The myth that death robs us of life will have died long ago. The anguish of bereavement and the fear of falling off the end of a flat Earth will seem equally ridiculous.

Sons and daughters of God will come and go from the Earth with purpose. Disease has no power over the unfettered flow of Divine Life. We will leave upon our realization of completion. And leaving the Earth will not separate us from our loved ones who remain.

Not all will feel the need to visit Earth in physical body.

We will be aware of their etheric presence when their attention is with us. We will be aware of other orders of spiritual beings, commune with them, and cherish their sacred work in our realm.

We will know that Earth, our host, is alive. We will join our minds with her and exchange blessings. We will grasp with gratefulness the radiant love of another order of life that we call our Sun.

Throughout it all, we will be immersed in the One Presence and One Power that exists throughout the universe. Talking with God will be commonplace. Just as the workstation computer consults the mainframe, we will consult Universal Mind on everything.

And then there is the human mind net. Oneness brings a total lack of privacy. We will share our every thought on an e-mail that is addressed to everyone. Surfing the mind net will bring us great satisfaction as well as information. The power of "we" is always greater than the sum of the parts.

Those who incarnate into Earth will do so in order to experience the glories of the physical world at great depth. We will not withdraw from physical experience—just its limitations. Telepathy will often replace spoken language, though we will preserve use of voice for the magnificent art of vibrating our world to change the texture of physical reality.

Spiritual travel will fill the need to roam far places. But our greatest rewards will come from mundane, creative physical experiences. Touch will be cherished as sacred. Families will love and caress while being part of the greater family of the whole.

Gardeners will pass energy to the soil with their hands and

bless the plants with the energy of their hearts, growing enough bounty for all. Cooks will prepare physical nourishment, adding the spiritual energies that will enrich it.

Some physical labor will be performed for the joy of experiencing it. Other labors will be accomplished with the advanced powers of mind. Physical sports and challenges will flourish for the depth of experience they convey. We will swim to the depths of the sea, climb the highest mountains, and sail on the wind without airplanes.

Music, art, motion, sculpture, writing, theater, carpentry, and fabrication will take a multitude of creative forms. Scientists will explore the inner essence of every aspect of this physical world, using their minds as their main research instrument.

This reality may seem far away, but it's not as far as you might think. Certain aspects of this abstract dream are quite close.

A BEGINNING . . .

For example, shortly we will create and live the dreams planted in our souls through use of mental imagery and communion with God. Abundance, healing, guidance, and harmony with the Earth are only a short reach once we harness those higher energies that we spiritual explorers are pursuing.

We are here to usher in the beginning of the transition. We stand with one foot in the past and the other poised for a leap of faith. The contributions we could make seem so small and insignificant. Yet the possibilities before us are filled with power.

We are the Wright brothers, hoping to sail above the ground for a few hundred yards after years of work. Jet planes and space stations are not very far behind. We are more capable of bringing change to this planet than we have ever realized.

I believe that in future Earth, historical analysis of our era will read something like this:

"The people of the early twenty-first century were still primitives in that they did not know how to use the energies of Mind and Heart to take command of their physical limitations. Thus they were enslaved to the physical world.

"But an adventurous few set out in search of the inner potentials that we presently consider commonplace.

"Against a backdrop of tremendous human ignorance, these few still managed to cut through their limits in enough different areas to begin to form a picture of humankind's next step in evolution.

"They opened the door, and the generations who followed went in and colonized this new realm of higher human potential.

"These spiritual explorers were a vanguard that fought hard for little pieces of the higher realm, which we take for granted today. Yet, without them, humankind might never have taken the leap, and we might still be in bondage to the physical world."

Speaking for myself, I wish to be counted among those "adventurous few." How about you?

ABOUT THE AUTHOR

Robert Lee Marshall was born in Kentucky on June 5, 1950, and grew up in Ohio. His father was a Methodist minister who eventually left the traditional church looking for something deeper. This gave Robert the opportunity to become acquainted with Unity at the age of fifteen when his whole family discovered the New Thought Unity Center in Cincinnati.

A trained hypnotist by the age of thirteen, Bob Marshall graduated from high school top of his class in science and math. He attended Rensselaer Polytechnic Institute in Troy, New York, for two years, followed by a year at Glendale College in Glendale, California, pursuing a degree in chemical engineering. A crisis of "purpose" led him to leave college and head into Unity ministry. To this day he considers himself to be a "spiritual engineer," charting the most efficient techniques of tapping into higher potential.

Bob entered Unity ministerial school a year after his father became a Unity minister. Bob was ordained in 1973 at the age of twenty-three and has since served Florida churches in Miami, Venice, Fort Pierce, and Orlando. Presently, he is senior minister of Unity Church of Christianity in Orlando. From 1997 to 1999, Bob served as president of Unity's Southeast Region.

The Reverend Marshall has been deeply involved in the

spiritual retreat experience throughout his ministry. He is a spiritual explorer and his yearning for a deep spiritual experience has led him through a number of mystical traditions even while serving as a Unity minister. He has studied Yoga meditation techniques, become a Sufi initiate, and explored Native-American shamanism. In recent years Bob has brought a condensation of all of his exploration back to a concentration on his roots in Unity. His commitment to spiritual *experience*, not mere philosophy, highlights for him the mystical side of the Unity movement. Much like Charles and Myrtle Fillmore before him, he hopes to empower everyone to open the doors to higher experience within themselves.

Bob Marshall lives on 2¾ acres near Orlando with his wife Karrin and daughter Lindsey Rose, who is the light of his life. His two grown stepsons, Joshua and Damean, live nearby. Bob is an avid gardener and is nurturing over a hundred fruit trees and berry bushes on his property including both tropical and subtropical varieties. He loves traveling, home remodeling, being involved in all types of nature activities, and going on "an adventure." His most valuable time is often spent at home doing something mundane. He explains, "Real life experienced at a heightened level of awareness is the most exciting thing we can do!"

Printed in the U.S.A.   188-2840-5M-5-01